DATE D

THE NATION'S CHILDREN

in three volumes

THE NATION'S CHILDREN

Edited by Eli Ginzberg

1: THE FAMILY AND SOCIAL CHANGE

Committee on Studies

Published 1 9 6 0 for the Golden Anniversary

White House Conference on Children and Youth

by COLUMBIA UNIVERSITY PRESS, NEW YORK

GOLDEN ANNIVERSARY
WHITE HOUSE CONFERENCE ON
CHILDREN AND YOUTH

HONORARY CHAIRMAN
The President of the United States
Dwight D. Eisenhower

HONORARY VICE CHAIRMAN
The Secretary of Health, Education, and Welfare
Arthur S. Flemming

CHAIRMAN
Mrs. Rollin Brown

VICE CHAIRMEN

Hurst R. Anderson
Philip S. Barba, M.D.
Mrs. James E. Blue
Robert E. Bondy
Erwin D. Canham
Donald K. David
Luther Foster
Msgr. Raymond J. Gallagher

Mrs. Frank Gannett
Edward D. Greenwood, M.D.
Daryl P. Harvey, M.D.
Donald S. Howard
Ruth A. Stout
Rabbi Marc H. Tanenbaum
Rev. Dr. William J. Villaume

SECRETARY
Mrs. Katherine B. Oettinger

ASSOCIATE DIRECTOR
Isabella J. Jones

EXECUTIVE DIRECTOR
Ephraim R. Gomberg

COMMITTEE ON STUDIES
Chairman: Eli Ginzberg *

Leona Baumgartner, M.D.
Mrs. Fitzhugh W. Boggs
Mrs. Wright W. Brooks
Sister Mary de Lourdes *
Jack R. Ewalt, M.D.
Mrs. Otto L. Falk
Mrs. David Graham
Margaret Hickey
Reuben L. Hill, Jr.*
A. John Holden
Rt. Rev. Arthur Carl
  Lichtenberger

Harry M. Lindquist
Mrs. Alvin A. Morrison
Captain Frank J. Popello
William L. Pressly
Milton J. E. Senn, M.D.*
Joseph Stokes, M.D.*
Ruth A. Stout *
Rabbi Marc H. Tanenbaum *
John Tannehill
Ralph W. Tyler *
Whitney M. Young, Jr.*

* Member of the Steering Committee.

PREFACE

THE PLAN for these three volumes was developed by the Steering Committee of the Committee on Studies for the Golden Anniversary White House Conference for Children and Youth at its meetings early in 1959. The Steering Committee quickly decided that it should not seek to stimulate new research for the Conference since the results could not possibly be available before the convening of the delegates in March, 1960. It recognized, however, the desirability of providing the delegates with materials that would help to outline the major developments in the field of children and youth since the 1950 Conference and would provide a basis for charting directions for the next decade.

These volumes were designed to meet this twofold purpose. The speedy approval by the Taconic Foundation of a grant to cover the expenses involved in preparing the materials, and assistance from other foundations to facilitate their distribution, proved a major boon, and grateful acknowledgment is hereby made of these generous and constructive contributions.

The Steering Committee set high goals for these volumes: contributors were to be recognized experts in their respective fields; they were to write for the educated layman; not for the specialist; the contributors were to strive for balance and eschew extremes; they were to limit themselves to about 5,000 words; and their essays were to be in hand by September, so that the published volumes could be sent to the delegates at least two months before the Conference.

These ambitious objectives could not have been met had it not been for the splendid cooperation of the contributors. Only one person who accepted an assignment failed to complete it and then only for reasons of health.

Most contributors recommended a limited number of books and articles that are more or less readily available so that an interested reader can pursue any subject further. These recommendations have been consolidated into a reading list appended to each volume.

The observant reader may be perplexed by differences in the figures cited. For instance, one author uses $4,800 and another $5,000 as average family income for 1957. Still another refers to average family income as being "well over $6,000 in 1958." The difference between $4,800 and $5,000 reflects a rounding off of median total income. The "well over $6,000" figure reflects primarily the use of the mean as an average and a more complete coverage of income, including an estimate of the value of income in kind. In general, differences reflect choices as to dates, sources, and averages. It should be emphasized that each author is responsible for the selection of his material and its interpretation.

The willingness of the Columbia University Press to accept a very difficult schedule and its success in meeting it warrants special note.

Ruth Szold Ginzberg helped to style the three volumes for press under great pressure of time, and contributed significantly to their readability.

Robert W. Smuts, Research Associate of the Conservation of Human Resources Project, Columbia University, read the galleys carefully and made helpful suggestions which led to many clarifications.

Eli Ginzberg, CHAIRMAN
COMMITTEE ON STUDIES
THE GOLDEN ANNIVERSARY WHITE HOUSE
CONFERENCE ON CHILDREN AND YOUTH

CONTENTS

INTRODUCTION

by ELI GINZBERG

THE WORKING TITLE for this, the first of three volumes on *The Nation's Children*, was "Perspective"—a term that conveys the general purpose and intent in assembling this distinguished group of contributions even if it fails to specify the focus of their concern and treatment. The revised title, "The Family and Social Change," provides this focus. It further suggests that the contributors have looked at the United States and its children with a wide lens in order to delineate the major changes and have forsaken detail.

What perspective do these essays provide on the family and social change? In brief review, we find Professor Dulles reminding us that at the turn of the century the farm and the small town still played a major part in shaping the quality of American life, while today it is the suburb that has preempted this role. The magnitude of this transformation is further underscored by Professor Gottmann whose entire

Eli Ginzberg is Director of the Conservation of Human Resources Project, Director of Staff Studies of the National Manpower Council, and Professor of Economics at Columbia University.

essay is devoted to the impact of urbanization. He deals at length with the complex problems of Megalopolis, but he insists that the city, even the giant city, can continue to be a force for good if its citizens will face up intelligently and forthrightly to the problems which it creates, as well as to the opportunities which it presents.

Dr. Bernert demonstrates that among the reasons for the very rapid growth of large metropolitan areas is the large-scale increase in population which has been under way ever since the outbreak of World War II, when the declining birthrate of the 1930s was dramatically reversed. Within the single decade of 1950–1960, the rate of increase in the number of children was almost twice as large as that of the total population. She points out that one consequence of this increase will be the pressure on the schools to absorb during the 1960s about 15 million *additional* pupils.

Much of the explanation for the more recent changes on the demographic front lies in the remarkable performance of the American economy, which, as Professor Abramovitz tells us, is today providing an income for the average family in excess of $6,000. With jobs easy to get, more and more young people marry at an early age and start their families early. They feel secure about their personal future. They are not forced to choose, as did their fathers and grandfathers, between getting a start in their career and getting married. They can do both.

This feeling of personal security about the future has un-doubtedly been further strengthened and re-enforced by the amazing reduction in infant and childhood illness and mor-tality. As Dr. Rosen reminds us, as late as 1885, more than 1 out of every 4 infants died within the first year of birth. To-day's rate is less than 3 out of 100! Of the many factors which contributed to achieving these and other health gains, an important one has been the growing power of the economy which made possible the expansion of services both in the public and the private sectors. The best index of recent medical progress is Dr. Rosen's identification of the problems that still await solution—perinatal mortality, the prevention of human malformation, and improvements in mental health. These are a far cry from the health challenges at the turn of the century.

It is now generally acknowledged that it is neither desirable nor practical to consider problems of children without setting many if not all of them within the complex of the family, which is both the first and the most important of all institutions concerned with their nurture. Many lost sight of this simple fact in recent decades in their enthusiasm for one or another form of social gadgeteering. The preeminence of the family in this context explains why this volume contains three specific contributions on this subject.

Professor Arensberg has delineated what is universal and what is unique about the American family in his comprehensive overview of the structure and functioning of the family in different societies. He describes the extent to which the American family is largely restricted to the "biological" unit of father, mother, and minor children, in contrast to the very large joint-family of India and China or the stem-family, somewhat more limited in size, typical of many peasant communities in Western Europe and elsewhere.

Professor Hill sharpens the focus on the American family

by emphasizing the continuities and changes that have characterized it during the past several decades. His review
stresses such significant trends as the increasing proportion
of the total population that marries, and this, he says, is
not unconnected with the relatively high divorce rate. In Professor Hill's opinion, perhaps the most important trend in
the contemporary American family is the redefinition of
marital and parental roles and functions.

Dr. Hylan Lewis, in his appraisal of the changes that are
occurring in the Negro family, provides still another dimension for understanding the continuing transformation of the
American family. He points out the new task of the Negro
family as it seeks to prepare its members to live in a deseg-
regated world. The way in which the Negro family is shaped
by the city—both by its opportunities and deprivations—is
also illuminated. The salutary changes that are taking place
in the aspirations, participation, and tastes of the Negro family depend, in Dr. Lewis' opinion, first and foremost on the
broadened opportunities open to the Negro male in the job
market.

The penultimate essay on "The Place of Religion in
American Life" by the Very Rev. Monsignor Gallagher,
Rabbi Tanenbaum, and the Reverend Dr. Villaume warrants
special attention, since it represents one of the first, if not
the first, joint essay on religion by representatives of the three
major faiths in the United States. The essay is testimony to
the conviction expressed by the authors that "pointless differences which now dissipate the strength of religious influence in our country" should be eliminated. The authors

clarify the major role of religion in the growth of this nation, and they set forth the need and the opportunity for religion to play an active role in strengthening contemporary life.

The last essay, by August Heckscher, helps to frame the order of change that has been taking place in American society by emphasizing the inroads that leisure has made into our work-oriented life. He points out that as the pattern of adult life shifts increasingly from work to leisure activities, it cannot fail to exercise a major impact on youth whose values and behavior are inevitably shaped by the world into which they must fit themselves. Mr. Heckscher reassures us that the new leisure is bringing the two worlds of adult and youth closer together. But he warns us that while leisure provides an opportunity for the expansion and deepening of personality, it does not guarantee it.

These brief paragraphs have had a modest aim—to whet the reader's appetite and to indicate the richness of the materials contained in these ten essays.

A recent personal experience underscored for me the order of change in the contemporary world. Upon my return from Princeton, where I had lectured, I told my seven-year-old son about Einstein, who had lived there. I set forth Einstein's theory of relativity as best I could, and then told him that, curiously, Einstein had had difficulty with simple arithmetic: he counted and re-counted his change on a trolley car. My son's face clouded over—he had had no difficulty in following my explanation of the theory of relativity, but he exploded with the question, "What's a trolley car?"

THE NATION'S CHILDREN

1: THE FAMILY AND SOCIAL CHANGE

FROM FRONTIER TO SUBURBIA

by FOSTER RHEA DULLES

IN THE YEARS that have stretched from the close of the nineteenth century to the present—the years that one historian has characterized as those of "The Big Change"—there have been far-reaching transformations in every phase of American life. Of course transformations characterize every period of history. What has so dramatically distinguished the first half of the twentieth century, however, is the extreme rapidity of change. The amazing acceleration of scientific and technological advance has made over the face of America and had momentous consequences in industry, in agriculture, in transportation, and in the waging of modern war.

These developments have also revolutionized American home life. Never within so short a span of time have the conditions affecting family relations, and both the problems and the opportunities in bringing up children, changed so drastically. Young people today face an entirely different world from that which their parents, let alone their grand-

Foster Rhea Dulles is Professor of American History at The Ohio State University.

parents, knew in their youth. They take for granted scientific marvels that only a relatively few years ago were hardly envisaged. Their ways of life and their sense of values are founded upon circumstances and premises which are greatly different from those that governed the generation preceding theirs—to the continued confusion and at times consternation of their parents.

It is only since the beginning of the present century that electric power has invaded the home and made possible the myriad machines and gadgets that characterize modern housekeeping. The automobile which has given such incredible physical mobility to the American people was an erratic and very expensive plaything of the rich less than sixty years ago. Travel by air, which has now become so commonplace that even the introduction of jets causes hardly a ripple of excitement, did not begin until the Wright brothers made their first flight at Kitty Hawk as recently as 1903. The movies were no more than the faintly flickering images of the vitascope at the opening of the century, and the immensely significant experiments in the field of communications which introduced radio and television were brought to fruition in the last forty years.

These so recent developments of technology, together with many others, have contributed not only to a higher standard of living, greater leisure, and broader opportunities for a full and satisfying life than any people have ever before known, but also to many of the stresses and strains of present-day living. They have created problems that not only seriously affect our domestic economy and foreign relations, but every phase of day-by-day family life and the always difficult adjustments of youth to the society in which they live.

What are the responsibilities of children when household tasks are in some instances immensely simplified by modern gadgets, and in more wealthy families seemingly complicated by the substitution of machines for servants? How can playtime be most advantageously used against the background of a recreational pattern revolutionized by the movies, television, and the automobile? How can discipline be upheld under conditions which make for so much individual freedom for young people and often seem to encourage license? In what ways can children be most effectively trained and educated to play their future role in a society wherein manners, customs, and values are subject to the constant assault of technological advances so rapid that adjustment can hardly hope to keep up with them?

Herein lies the challenge of how the present adult population can most effectively promote the opportunities that will enable today's children and youth "to realize their full potentialities for a creative life in freedom and dignity."

An Industrial Society

The basic underlying change reflecting this growth of technology that America has experienced in the modern era has been the transformation from an agricultural to an industrial community. This is clearly apparent not only in the constant expansion in manufactures but in the rise of industrial towns and cities. Even farming itself has tended to become a business rather than a way of life under the impact of these industrial forces. The twentieth century has produced a vastly different economic structure for the nation from that which characterized the nineteenth century.

Until relatively recent times a major factor in our national growth was still the frontier—the frontier as both symbol and actuality. It represented free land, an expanding agricultural community, and an ever beckoning opportunity for new settlers on the western prairies. It was only in 1890 that the Census reports officially announced that the frontier, described as an unbroken line of western settlement, had finally disappeared. Even then there remained vast areas of free land still to be taken, and agricultural expansion would continue into the new century. But a great epoch in our national history came to a close when the traditional frontier disappeared; the future clearly belonged to industry rather than agriculture, to the city rather than to the farm.

This shift in emphasis soon began to have far-reaching effects. It had its political as well as its economic and social implications. A dramatic instance was the election of 1896 when William Jennings Bryan, who more than any other political leader of the day represented the agrarian interests of the country, went down to defeat before William McKinley, the spokesman of big business and industry. Sang Vachel Lindsay:

> Defeat of the wheat.
> Victory of the letterfiles
> And plutocrats in miles
> With dollar signs upon their coats.[1]

[1] From *Bryan, Bryan, Bryan, Bryan*. Copyright 1914. Quoted with permission of The Macmillan Company.

The victory for industry and the city can also be illustrated by the movement of population that took place in the ensuing years and by the occupational shifts within the labor force. Between 1890 and 1930, the number of people living in communities with more than 2,500 persons rose from about one-third to something more than one-half the total population. Another twenty years and the urban population was nearly two-thirds of the total. This trend has continued through the 1950s.

This change from a rural to an urban America is also shown by the employment statistics. Out of the total number of employed civilians in 1958, approximately 58 million were engaged in nonagricultural activities and only 6 million in farming.

These are broad generalizations about significant trends but their potential effect on the nation's youth is readily apparent. Whereas a half century or more ago, the traditions and mores of the farm, the village, or the small town greatly influenced family relationships and the position of children in the home, urban and suburban standards have come to supersede them almost completely. Something of the old simplicity and informality of life has been lost in the mounting complexity of a society that centers about the city. Even for children still brought up in rural communities, the quiet—sometimes deadening monotony—of isolated farm life has given way to the more rapid pace of modern living, while in the urban communities—and suburbs—there is no escaping the consequences of today's crowded, congested conditions.

More Equitable Income

As this new industrial urban America has developed, a
further significant change affecting family life has been an
increasing and more equitably distributed national income.
This trend has been most pronounced in very recent years,
particularly since the depression of the '30s. For the first time
in our history the great majority of wage earners, as well as
white-collar workers and other better-paid members of the
labor force, are able to purchase the wide range of products
that they themselves are producing. This was not generally
the case in the 1890s. America was then engaged in the
rapid expansion of basic industry, financed in part through
the export of agricultural products and raw materials. By
1914, when Henry Ford raised the base wage of his employees to $5 a day, the consumer durable goods industries
were becoming an important part of the economy and a
few far-sighted businessmen had begun to recognize that
high wages were the foundation for a growing domestic
market. The constant pressure of militant labor unions, especially since the mid-1930s, has also helped to bring about a
great change in this regard. Wage earners now make up the
great bulk of the consumer market, not only for food and
clothing, but for the automobiles, the refrigerators, the television sets that have become the staples of American life.

The statistical evidence of the increase in wages, and the
consequent phenomenal rise in the standard of living for the
American people as a whole, is often confusing. It has to be
related to changes in the price level and to changes in the

quality of goods. In very general terms, however, real wages —that is wages adjusted to the price level—rose only moderately in the period from 1897 to 1914, about one-half of 1 percent annually. In the latter year it was estimated that anywhere from one-third to one-half the labor force were still earning less than enough to support their families in decent conditions. The war and postwar years saw more substantial gains; the depression of 1929–33 then reversed the trend with not only wage cuts but spiralling unemployment. Since then however, the upward pace in real earnings has not only been renewed but greatly accelerated. Between 1939 and 1950, real earnings for production workers in the field of manufacturing, for example, rose more than 40 percent, and they were further supplemented in many instances by old-age pensions and other fringe benefits largely unknown in earlier periods.

Current figures show that average earnings for such workers had risen to about $90 weekly in 1959, while a comprehensive study showed that the median family income from wages and salaries in the United States was $4,800 in 1957. In these circumstances the American people as a whole have been able to spend an increasingly greater proportion of their income on nonessentials, and often luxuries, beyond anything to which previous generations could aspire.

Children no less than their parents have benefited from this phenomenal rise in living standards. It has in many cases freed them from traditional household tasks and chores, provided them new means of recreation or amusement (as will be subsequently considered in discussing the increased leisure in modern life), and in broad terms made their life easier and more free through greatly reducing child labor. In addition very significantly increased family incomes have made possible a longer term in school or college for the great majority of the nation's young people. While there would seem to be little change in the accepted tradition of young people seeking to earn money for themselves as soon as possible, the improved economic status of their parents has enabled them to use such earned money for their own purposes rather than contribute it entirely for household expenses.

Other Changes

There have been many other changes in the pattern of American life importantly affecting the family and children. The twentieth century has witnessed immense gains in people's health. Education has expanded greatly in response to new needs and new demands. There have been developments within the broad field of religion affecting people's attitude toward manners and morals and altering the place of the church in family life. From a quite different angle, the participation of the United States in two world wars has had important repercussions on the attitudes and mores of young people especially. It is necessary only to recall the revolt of the younger generation in the 1920s, the strange manifestations of the Jazz Age, the effects of worldwide overseas service during World War II, and the confusing consequences of today's continued compulsory service in the armed forces.

HEALTH. The nation's improved physical well-being, resulting from both medical advance and more effective measures in the area of public health, may perhaps be especially singled out. This is often forgotten in the somewhat complacent attitude that prevails in an age when so many of the diseases of the past have been almost entirely eradicated. And this is true for children to an extent that would have seemed miraculous to earlier generations. This is not to suggest that disease and ill-health do not remain important problems for modern society. Of course they do. But medicine and public health research have won victories even more significant than those of engineering and industrial technology.

The tremendous gains in reducing infant mortality, the successful attacks that have been made upon the diseases of childhood, the improvement in child health due to inoculations and sanitary precautions, the emphasis upon more healthy dietary procedures—these are among the most significant developments of the modern age for children. Whatever may be said of other consequences of scientific advance, those that may be attributed to medicine would appear to be wholly beneficial for young people as well as for society as a whole.

It may be that the tensions of the modern world have an adverse effect upon the emotional stability of children as well as adults, and are responsible for problems that earlier generations did not encounter. But physical health is better and life expectancy greatly increased. It remains an amazing fact

that the American child born today has a life expectancy of
some seventy years—nearly twenty-five years more than that
of the child born in the rural America of the 1890s.

BIRTH RATE. At the same time, changes in the birth rate
have had important consequences for family life. Over the
past half century there has been a pronounced trend with
one sharp fluctuation. The steady decline which continued
until the mid-1930s led to anguished cries of possible race
suicide. Since World War II, however, the birth rate increase has been a surprising and notable phenomenon—the
number of births per 1,000 of population has risen from
approximately 18 to 25. Earlier marriages, a conspicuous fact
of life on university campuses throughout the country, and
the apparent desire of young couples to have more offspring,
are primarily responsible for this reversal of the long-time
trend. Today's children have more siblings than their parents
generally had and thus at least the opportunity for a more
emotionally satisfying life within the family circle.

EDUCATION. Relatively more children now attend school
than ever before, starting at an earlier age and leaving at a
later age. The total enrollment in public schools, indeed, has
more than doubled since the beginning of the century, with
the greatest growth at the two ends of the public education
system—the high schools and the kindergartens. The estimated totals for 1958 show over 33 million pupils in public
schools out of a population of 42 million between the ages
of five and seventeen years.

The problems of education are today more important than
ever before because of this great increase in pupil enrollment

and because of the demands of an industrialized society. This is not the place to discuss the complicated issues that have arisen in regard to popular support for such an expanded school system, the educational philosophy of the country, the continuing debate over curricula and teaching methods. What is every year more apparent, however, is the mounting interest in providing as much education for children as possible. The growth of kindergartens perhaps reflects a desire for institutional help in caring for the very young rather than educational zeal, but the emphasis upon the high school and college reflects the need for more training—whether it is vocational, professional, or liberal—in our highly organized modern society.

RECREATION. Another important aspect of change is the increased leisure time in modern society which, as previously suggested, both directly and indirectly affects children quite as much as adults.

Indeed this increase in leisure is surely one of the most significant social changes of the twentieth century. Its impact upon the families of wage earners is even greater than upon the families of others in the labor force. Sixty years ago the working-week for industrial employees might be as much as eighty hours; today the average is forty hours. While the reduction for other business employees, and especially for the self-employed and the professional classes, has been not nearly so substantial, they have nevertheless benefited very much from the trend toward longer holidays and paid vacations.

The housewife has also found increased leisure through

the introduction of labor-saving devices in the home. The new laundering machines, vacuum cleaners, refrigerators, dish washers, electric mixers, and a host of other gadgets have helped to relieve her of a great deal of the drudgery of the past. All this may not be an unalloyed blessing, and science has not yet developed a reliable machine for baby care, but the homekeeper can find time that was never available in the average family before the advent of the mechanized kitchen.

The consequences of this increased leisure, however, are often contradictory so far as they affect family life and the position of children. For the same technology that has increased leisure has also multiplied the possible uses of leisure. Parents have more free hours to be with their children, but they are at the same time drawn out of the home by the automobile, the movies, and spectator sports. And arrayed against such new outside opportunities for recreation and amusement, there is the opposing force of radio and television. It would be impossible to determine in any really significant way the extent to which these manifestations of the machine age tend to include or exclude children from family life in comparison with the pre-automobile and pre-television era. One thing, however, is certain: family life and parent-children relationships have greatly altered as a consequence of the availability of these recreational activities, which were unknown at the century's opening.

Circumstances in this respect differ—as they alway must—according to the economic and social status of the family. For children of families with lower incomes, the reduction of household tasks through mechanized housekeeping may make for a more satisfying life with greater time for both study and play, or it may actually disrupt family harmony if the parents irresponsibly use the new leisure. In the upper middle classes, a quite different situation prevails. For here the disappearance of servants, a consequence of both economic change and the restriction of immigration, is a phenomenon for which mechanized housekeeping is only partial compensation. The children of such families may actually have more household chores than previously, demanding accommodation and adjustment of a quite different nature than in lower income homes.

Among middle class families, moreover, the want of servants has brought about other changes in social life and in modes of entertainment. It has contributed, together with the experience of prohibition days, to the rise of the cocktail party as a fashionable institution which lightens the burden of more formal entertaining. But even then the servantless families in this strata of society face the problem of who is to take care of the children when the parents go out. Its solution, a practice unknown to earlier generations, is the employment of a baby sitter.

The social and recreational life of the children themselves in this modern age may in some instances pattern itself after that of their parents. This obtains at least to the extent that they jointly use the newly developed agencies of amusement. When children are included in motor trips and vacation tours, go to the movies with their parents, or find television a common entertainment, the result may be the development of more common interests. But different interests often make mutual activities difficult. Where to drive, what movie to see, what television program to watch may make for conflict and controversy rather than greater accord within the family circle.

The importance of radio and television in family life is found in both the newness and the broad scope of these new agencies of mass entertainment. The first radio programs which were heard by a handful of wondering listeners equipped with what today would be considered antique head phones were broadcast just forty years ago. Today it is estimated that some 53 million homes have radios. Moreover countless households have more than one radio and they are built into most automobiles—to a grand total of 155 million radio sets for the country as a whole. Television lags behind these figures but the number of home sets is rapidly catching up and the current total is estimated at 50 million. The promoters of the electronics industry, indeed, suggest in some of their more enthusiastic estimates that there are actually more homes with radio and television than the total number of homes reported by the Census Bureau! However this may be, statistics are hardly necessary to illustrate the popularity of radio and television for the families of present-day America.

The influence of television upon children is incalculable. Whether it is in some ways good, whether it is altogether bad, whether it is destroying the child's independence and creativity by making reading a lost art and dulling youthful sensibilities, or whether it is stimulating and healthful, opening up new vistas upon the world, television is playing a tremendously significant role in setting up the values of a child's universe and in molding his attitudes.

A danger that is often pointed out, for both adults and children, is the part both radio and television have had in impressing uniformity upon American life. It is charged that the omnipresent commercials tend to force upon society patterns of behavior that are destroying the individuality of an earlier age, and that herein lies one of the greatest changes in American society since the days still symbolized by the frontier. In the case of children, who are particularly susceptible to all influences making for conformity, television does often appear to spell out attitudes from which the child departs at his peril. The first of these is the compulsion to watch television. And then there are all the behavior patterns which television suggests as the accepted norm for well-adjusted boys and girls. Somewhat ironically, in the light of complaints that the freedom and individualism of frontier days have been lost, it might be noted that the popularity of Westerns remains one of the most intriguing features of television programming. Witness how the child world can be swept by such a craze as the Davy Crockett fad!

The more traditional forms of recreation for children have also undergone marked changes as a consequence of the new circumstances of modern life. The trend is away from simple, spontaneous activities to more formal organized sports and games. The casual vacant lot baseball game has given way to the little leagues; the old swimming hole has been replaced by the community pool. In fulfillment of their obligations to their children, modern parents tend more and more to rely upon arranging for their participation in various forms of highly organized activity. This reflects perhaps a comparable trend in the adult world toward the professionalization of sports and even "spectatoritis" as a substitute for active play. In any event, play today is regulated and controlled to an extent that earlier generations—on the farm, in the country—could hardly have imagined.

A NATION ON WHEELS. A further change in family life has been brought about by the automobile. Its role obviously extends far beyond the field of recreation, for both parents and children. While motoring for pleasure constitutes a large part of the use of the automobile, no single product of the technological revolution has had more far-ranging consequences on every aspect of American living. The cars parked about factories, places of business, and shopping centers, our crowded highways and congested city streets, offer constant and incontrovertible evidence of a complete dependence upon the automobile in present-day society.

The visual evidence of the number of cars on the roads is amply supported by the statistics: there were some 78 million motor vehicles in the United States in 1958—more than twice the number for as recent a year as 1940. Including bus and truck drivers, nearly 80 million persons (almost half the country's population) were licensed to drive. In the perspective of history, there may be something astounding about such figures, but they can be readily accepted by anyone who has had occasion to motor on a summer weekend in almost any part of the country.

The automobile provides a basic means of transportation in business and industry, entirely apart from the role of trucks and buses; it has served to link the country and the city by breaking down the one-time isolation of the farm, and it has greatly widened the horizons of the American people through holiday trips and vacation travel throughout the country. But the automobile has affected the world of children quite as much as the adult world. It has caused the general disappearance of the Little Red School House and substituted the new consolidated schools. It has made possible the convenient transportation of children for a host of social activities that were impracticable in the pre-automobile era. It has given teen-agers an independence and freedom of movement (when they are able to obtain use of the family car or somehow buy their own second-hand jalopies) which their counterparts in earlier generations never knew.

But the automobile has consequently created a host of problems as well as providing so many obvious benefits. Questions revolving about the use of the family car by the young, the age at which driving licenses should be granted, practical precautions to minimize the hazards of reckless driving, possible safeguards for manners and morals in the broad area of adolescent dating, point up only some of the issues which the motorizing of America has created.

Suburbia

A final development in our evolving twentieth-century civilization which importantly influences family life and children is one that is at once a consequence of the technological revolution of our times and also brings together and exemplifies many of its most distinctive features. This is the growth of suburbia. There are still millions of persons living on farms or in small villages; there are many more living in thriving industrial towns or big cities. But the growth of the suburbs clustering about our great urban centers is once again altering the face of America. The number of metropolitan areas has itself increased in the past two decades, but the suburbs embraced within their geographic limits have grown much more rapidly than the central cities themselves. In some cases, for example New York, there has actually been a decline in the city population while that of the surrounding area has increased enormously. The new garden apartments in the city's outskirts, the workers' housing developments, the more expensive suburbs away from city limits—these are increasingly distinctive features of the national landscape.

Suburbs themselves are not new. But those of an earlier day were restricted by the existing means of transportation: railroads and suburban trolley lines. The automobile has made possible their extension farther and farther into the countryside by providing the means to take the head of the family from home to railway station, if not the entire way to factory or office. It is in the world of suburbia, indeed, that the automobile is really indispensable. It transports the children to school and conveys the housewife to her supermarket and shopping center. It provides not only a popular form of recreation in itself, but enables the family to go to those places where they may either play themselves or watch others play. It is the very basis of the suburb's strange and wonderful life.

These growing communities still attract primarily members of the business and professional classes, salesmen and distributors, white-collar workers. Nevertheless the improving economic status of wage earners has made it possible for an ever larger number of families in this category to seek out the relatively greater open spaces and broader benefits for children that suburban developments offer in comparison with towns and cities. They are a compromise answer to the conflicting pulls of city and country which is designed to meet the housing problems posed by an industrialized society. Carefully graded according to economic and social status, with homes ranging from two-room apartments to split-level ranch houses, embodying all the features of the technological revolution, suburbs are more and more setting the standards and establishing the mores of our civilization. They are the pacemakers in the new culture and new value system of modern American society.

Nothing can suggest more graphically the contrast between the world in which today's children and young people are growing up and the world which the children and young people at the close of the past century confronted than a comparison of suburbia with that earlier period's small town. Neither are entirely typical of the society of their day. That is obvious. They are nevertheless contrasting symbols of how American culture has changed under the impact of technological advance in the past seventy years.

The small town of the 1890s, enveloped by its outlying farms, had a certain stability as well as leisurely atmosphere that even its counterpart today has largely lost. The spacious, comfortable houses with their deep yards and flowering gardens, set well back from quiet elm-shaded streets; the relatively little traffic, and that little composed of slow-moving wagons, carriages, buggies; the country stores that have been replaced by today's supermarkets and shopping centers—all this marked a quite different world than ours. Nor were the families who lived in these towns rushed and harried by the strident demands of a booming amusement industry which sought to mechanize—or at least profes-sionalize—every possible form of entertainment. The travel-ing theatre company, staging its performances at the local opera house, the Chatauqua meeting, the annual county fair, the occasional visit of the circus—"trailing clouds of glorified dust and filling our minds with the color of ro-mance," as Hamlin Garland has written—these were the only forms of recreation available to supplement village sports and games, church sociables, the meetings of the fraternal orders, and informal family visiting.

There was rarely any electricity, let alone refrigerators or deep freezes, in the comfortable homes along Main Street in the 1890s, and none whatsoever in rural areas; there were no automobiles (although the bicycle was becoming popular); there were no motion pictures, and no radio and no tele-vision; there were no multi-lane highways skirting the town or crisscrossing the countryside; there were no zooming jet planes to outrage the quiet air. Nor was there as yet any atomic bomb or any imaginings of the dangers of nuclear warfare!

And what of suburbia? The new real estate developments, whether vast housing projects for factory workers or more expensive, restricted middle-class subdivisions, have by their very nature a quality of sameness, are more uniform, than the towns and villages that grew up gradually in the past. They are congested and crowded as a consequence of a rapidly increasing population. An almost constant flow of traffic is a raucous interruption to everyday life, and the ubiquitous automobile, for all its benefits, emphasizes the hectic pace of suburban living. The shopping centers and supermarkets have a certain impersonality about them which contrasts sharply with the friendliness of the erstwhile local grocery store or meat market. If families have more actual leisure, there is still little of the leisurely atmosphere of earlier days. The suburbs are highly organized, for both adults and children, and present a pattern of living to which almost everyone is under heavy pressure to conform. There is often a competitive spirit in the air, giving a new urgency to the need "to keep up with the Joneses."

The children in these new communities may have greater educational opportunities than those in the small town of the 1890s, enjoy better health than those of earlier generations, have in some ways broader contacts, but they are also subject to pressures which have greatly changed the child's world. There is often no escape for them from the conventions and customs that circumscribe suburbia; it is more difficult for them than in the past to develop independence and individuality. The children living in this world of structured activities, more formalized recreation and amusement, and neighborhood prescribed conventions, may well be confused about their own individual responsibilities.

Family Life in a Complex Age

Looking back over the years, indeed, it is all too apparent that the scientific and technological revolution that has so rapidly carried the nation from an agrarian to an industrial society, from the frontier to suburbia, has brought with it highly divergent consequences for American family life. It has created a more "affluent society" than any other people have ever enjoyed, increased leisure beyond anything former generations envisaged, and opened up new possibilities for a richer and fuller life for all members of society. Yet to offset these actual or potential gains, this technological revolution has also greatly accelerated the pace of modern life, causing new stresses and strains in everyday living, and brought about a measure of crowding in city and even suburb that has immensely complicated all social organization.

This means ever new problems in family adjustment, in the relationship between parents and children, and in the direction of youth along the difficult path to maturity. Perhaps the basic issue is how young people can be brought up with a proper sense of responsibility in a situation that has freed them from so many of the obligations and duties that were theirs in a society that did not enjoy such a high standard of living and so many luxuries. Children today have a new freedom whose advantages and benefits are very real, but which obtain only if this freedom is held within reasonable bounds. Each generation must work out its own set of values in the light of changing circumstance. Something essential may well be lost, however, if such values do not remain fundamentally based upon principles that have grown out of established truths and past experience.

The continued rapidity of the changes taking place in modern society, even more than change in itself, remains the most complicating factor in the endless process of seeking to help children to adjust themselves, intellectually and emotionally, to the world in which they live. And with the potentialities for still further economic and social advance implicit in the discoveries relating to nuclear power (if the adult world somehow gains the wisdom to utilize such power for constructive rather than destructive purposes), there is little to suggest that the pace of technological progress is going to slow down.

We stand today on the threshold of a new age—the Age of Space. In some ways it is easier for children to accept this strange, new world than it is for their parents. Yet only so far as the older generation is able to realize how much—and how rapidly—the world has changed since its own youthful days, will it be in a position to help effectively today's children. Such understanding of both the past and the present is essential if society is to provide its young people with the guidance that will secure for them in an uncertain future a life of free and independent creative activity.

DEMOGRAPHIC TRENDS AND IMPLICATIONS

by ELEANOR H. BERNERT

KNOWLEDGE of the numbers of children and youth in the United States and their social and economic characteristics, as well as changes in numbers and characteristics, has been accumulating rapidly in the past several decades.[1] With the growth of knowledge has come considerable understanding of the problems of young people, resulting in a variety of programs and policies to meet their needs. A grasp of the demographic materials provides a basis and a perspective for the planning and implementation of many of these activities.

Though the responsibility for care of children in a democracy centers largely in the family, conscious effort and planning by both private and public agencies is predicated on the assumption that specific measures are required to as-

Eleanor H. Bernert is Associate Research Sociologist at the University of California at Los Angeles. This paper was prepared with the assistance of Sherri E. Cavan.

[1] Unless otherwise specified the data provided in this essay are derived from: U.S. Bureau of the Census, *Current Population Reports*, P-20, Nos. 32, 67, 84, 88, 93; P-25, Nos. 187, 193; P-50, Nos. 83, 87; P-60, No. 30.

sure that family needs are met and to provide opportunities for children essential for personal and social development. The rapid growth in the numbers of children, their increasing concentration in urban (and particularly suburban) centers, the new importance of the day care of children of working mothers are merely illustrative of changes emerging from the changing demographic structure of the nation.

The most recent comprehensive discussion of the demographic characteristics of young people, the interrelations of these characteristics and their probable future trends, summarized the available data from the turn of the century to 1950.[2] This essay will present only a brief review of the earlier analyses; the discussion will be focused upon the most recently available materials and the probable future trends with respect to the size and distribution of the nation's child and youth population, the changing ratio of children to adults of working age, the living and family arrangements of children, their educational and labor force participation, and the children of working mothers.

Ten years ago, on the occasion of the last White House conference on children and youth, the following demographic trends were noted: [3] 1) an upsurge in the child population; 2) an increase in the number of younger children and a decrease in the number of older children, with the most

[2] Eleanor H. Bernert, *America's Children* (New York: Wiley, 1958). See also Paul C. Glick, *American Families* (New York: Wiley, 1957); and Conrad Taeuber and Irene B. Taeuber, *The Changing Population of the United States* (New York: Wiley, 1958).

[3] Paul C. Glick, "Population Changes: Their Effect on Children and Youth." Paper presented at the Mid-century White House Conference on Children and Youth (mimeographed), Washington, 1950.

marked increase among children under five; 3) an accelerating trend toward urbanization and suburbanization; 4) though the largest number of children resided in the Southern states, considerable gains among children under five years of age in the Northeastern and Western states; 5) increasing migration of young children; 6) increasing elementary school and college enrollments and declining high-school enrollment; 7) an increase in part-time work among those attending school; 8) a shift among the older teen-agers to more responsible and remunerative jobs with concomitant increases in income; 9) an increasing propensity of older youths to leave parental homes; 10) most children living with relatives, usually both parents, though one-tenth living with only one parent; 11) improving economic levels of families with children.

Now, some ten years later we may summarize the intervening years as follows: 1) a continuing rise in the number of children, though leveling off among those under five, the earlier marked upsurge among the youngest shifting to an older group; 2) a continuation in the urbanization of children, though at a lower rate than formerly; 3) the largest number of children continuing to reside in the South, though considerable gains in the West and North Central states; 4) an upsurge in enrollment rates among five-year-olds (kindergarten), and for those in advanced high-school and college ages; 5) a considerable increase in part-time work among those attending school, reflecting both the expansion in the size of the school population and the continuing increasing propensity to work among students; 6) a continuation in the upgrading of the occupations among youth in the labor force, both those in the compulsory school ages and the older youth; 7) as in earlier years, most children living with relatives, primarily with both parents, though the number living with only one parent is increasing; 8) the economic levels of families with children continuing to improve, in some part due to the persistent increase in the number of working wives and mothers.

Growth in Numbers of Children

The number of children under eighteen years of age is estimated to have reached over 61 million in 1958 (the most recent estimate available at the time of writing, August 1959), an increase of almost 2 million children from the preceding year and an increase of almost 15 million from the date of the last census (1950). The rate of growth in the number of children from 1950 to 1958, over 30 percent, is twice as large as the comparable rate for the total population of all ages. Recent projections of the total number of children under eighteen for 1960 range from about 64 million to 65 million, representing a gain of about 35 to 40 percent from 1950. Comparable gains in the total population, which is estimated for 1960 at from 179 million to 181 million, amount to about 18 to 20 percent.

In contrast to the changes in the preceding decade when children under five showed the most marked increases, during the 1950s children of elementary school age (five to thirteen years) showed the most rapid gains. Within this age group there has been a shift in the growth rate from the younger to the older sectors of the group, due primarily to past fluctuations in the annual number of births. In recent years most of the increase occurred among the ten- to thirteen-year-olds, whereas in earlier years the five- to nine-year group represented most of the increase.

In 1958 there were over 31 million children in the elementary school ages as compared with 22 million in 1950, an increase of 40 percent. Children of preschool age (under five years old) numbered about 19.5 million in 1958 as compared with 16.1 million in 1950. Some of these preschool children of 1958 are already entering school; in the next few years close to 4 million children a year will become old enough to enter school for the first time. It is estimated that by 1960 the population of kindergarten age will reach almost 4 million, as compared with 2.7 million in 1950. Children of grade-school age, who numbered 19.5 million in 1950, will increase to about 29 million in 1960. An estimate of 21 million preschool children in 1960 appears reasonable.

Youths of high-school ages (fourteen to seventeen years) are approaching an all time peak; children born during the war are entering this age group, replacing the smaller number born during the prewar years. In 1958 the group numbered 10.6 million as contrasted with 8.4 million in 1950. It is estimated that the age group in 1960 will comprise about 11.5 million youths and that it will continue to grow for the next several years due to the sizable number of births during the late war and early postwar years, and will reach about 14 million by 1965.

The downward trend which was characteristic of the

college-age population (eighteen to twenty-one years) in earlier years (from the middle 1940s) came to an end in 1954, when small annual gains began to occur. In 1958 the group numbered about 9 million persons. It is estimated that this year (1960) the group numbers about 9.9 million. During the next several years it is anticipated that the age group will increase more rapidly as the larger number of young people who were born during the war and early postwar years enter the group, replacing the smaller number born during the closing years of the depression decade and the early years of the 1940 decade. By 1965 the number of youths aged eighteen to twenty-one years will reach about 12 million.

School Enrollment

School enrollment is to a large extent dependent upon customs which regulate who goes to school and for how long, and which relate to legal regulations about school attendance and labor force participation, the necessity and opportunity to find work, the availability of educational facilities, and progress made in advancing from one grade to the next in the usual age-grade cohorts. Increasingly in the United States factors enabling and encouraging children and youths to attend school have yielded mounting enrollment rates for almost all age groups. Thus have the combined effects of an expanding population and a steady rise in enrollment rates produced a phenomenal growth in the numbers of children and youth enrolled in the nation's schools: from about 30 million in 1950 to 34 million in 1953, 39 million in 1956, and 41 million in 1957. The total number of persons enrolled in the schools and colleges in the fall of 1958 was about 43 million. Approximately 2 million were in kindergarten, 28 million were in elementary school, 9.5 million were in high schools, and 3.2 million were enrolled in colleges and professional schools.

Enrollment rates among children of compulsory school age have already reached a maximum, while the peak in high school is yet to be realized. Between 1950 and 1958 the rise in enrollment rates was most marked for children five years of age, and only somewhat less pronounced for persons beyond compulsory school age. Among the five-year-olds, mostly because of a rise in kindergarten attendance, the percentage enrolled increased from 52 to 64 percent. For youths sixteen and seventeen years old the rates increased from 71 to 81 percent; and for those eighteen and nineteen years old the rates went up from 29 percent in 1950 to 38 percent in 1958. The rates also increased from 9 to 13 percent for persons twenty to twenty-four years old, and from 2 to 4 percent among those aged twenty-five to thirty-four years.

Rises in the enrollment rates have been common to both the white and nonwhite population, though in each age group nonwhite enrollment rates are below those for the white population.

Assuming the age enrollment rates of 1958 to prevail in 1960, it is estimated that there are over 31 million children of kindergarten and elementary school ages enrolled in school today. Among youths in the high-school ages there are over 10 million attending school. Two million youths eighteen and nineteen years old are enrolled in the nation's schools;

1.5 million are aged twenty to twenty-four years, and about another million are twenty-five to thirty-four years old.[4]

Projecting these rates ahead five years, population growth in the various age groups would yield enrollments of 34 to 35 million in the elementary school ages; 13 million in the high-school ages; about 2.5 to 3 million among the eighteen- and nineteen-year-olds; and 2.7 million aged twenty to thirty-four years.

Projecting these enrollment rates to 1970 (and assuming no decline in fertility, which would primarily affect the range shown for elementary school ages) would produce the following range of enrollment figures: 37 to 40 million in the elementary school ages; 14 million in the high-school ages; 3 million among the eighteen- and nineteen-year-olds; and 3 million twenty years of age or over.

Thus, assuming stability in the 1958 enrollment rates during the 1960s, we can expect that our schools must be prepared to absorb additional enrollments of about 8.5 million by 1965 and possibly 14 to 15 million by the end of the decade.

A recent analysis of the effect of demographic factors on school enrollment trends indicates the increasing importance of population change in determining school enrollment levels.[5] Enrollment rates are already maximized among chil-

[4] The United States Office of Education has estimated the 1959–60 enrollment at 46.5 million. These estimates are somewhat higher than those presented here due to differences in definitions, time references, enumeration methods, and our assumptions concerning enrollment rates.

[5] Charles B. Nam, "Demographic Factors in School Enrollment Trends, 1951–1958." Paper read at the Fifty-fourth Annual Meeting of the American Sociological Society, Chicago, September, 1959.

dren of elementary school ages; therefore, future gains in the size of this age group will determine the size of the population attending elementary school. At the high-school level enrollment rates have been increasing, especially for persons sixteen and seventeen years old. Mainly because of the increase in the size of the age group of high-school level, but also because of the continuing rise in enrollment rates, the number of youths enrolled in high school will continue to rise markedly. The largest relative gain in enrollment in future years will occur among the college ages. Enrollment rates have been rising most sharply in this age group, although they are still far below their demographic maximum. The age group itself will increase due to the larger number of persons born during the post-depression years and to the exit from the group of the relatively smaller number of depression-born persons. In summary, the future school and college enrollment levels will depend to a considerable extent upon the number of births in preceding years. Persons born during the persistent "baby boom" are already in all the various school levels and will continue to enter them; the future promises more rapidly rising school and college enrollment.

Dependency Ratios and Educational Expenditures

The rise in the birth rate in the past decade as well as the continuous expansion in life expectancy has resulted in mounting increases in the percentage of dependent population groups, while the percentage in the productive ages has declined. This trend toward an increasingly unfavorable balance between dependent and productive age groups became particularly marked during the 1940s. The past decade saw a continuation of this trend. In 1940 there were 1.67 persons of productive ages (eighteen to sixty-four years) for each dependent person aged under eighteen years or sixty-five years and over. By 1950 there were 1.56 persons of productive ages to each young or aged dependent person. The total dependency ratio in 1958 amounted to 1.31 producers per child or aged dependent. The ratios of productive persons to each dependent child, exclusive of the aged population, for 1940, 1950, and 1958 were 2.04, 1.96, and 1.50, respectively.

As in the past, urban populations enjoy a more favorable balance between dependent and productive age groups than do rural nonfarm and rural farm populations. In recent years there have been about 1.79 urban persons of productive age for each urban child under eighteen years of age, as contrasted with 1.32 and 1.28 for the rural nonfarm and rural farm populations, respectively. If the aged (sixty-five years and over) are added to the dependent children group, there is a ratio of 1.40 producers per dependent in urban areas, 1.11 in rural nonfarm areas, and 1.04 in rural farm areas.

As in earlier years, those states which are characterized by a high ratio of dependent to productive age persons are also characterized generally by relatively low family income, low expenditures for schooling, a low degree of urbanization, low educational attainment among adults, and poor educational performance.[6] Migration from areas of comparative disadvantage to areas of relatively greater opportunity makes the difference in the training and welfare services offered to young people in the various states a matter of nationwide concern. To the extent that public support for educational and welfare programs is derived chiefly from state resources, inequalities in state dependency loads and economic resources are particularly pertinent.

In the past decade, due to the rise in the number of births throughout the entire nation, each state has experienced an increase in the ratio of children to productive age persons. Generally those states which had the most favorable population age balance in 1950 again had the most favorable ratio in 1960. Similarly those states which experienced the least favorable child dependent-producer ratio in 1950 maintained the same comparative position in 1960. At both dates the most favorable demographic dependency burdens were found in the urban Northeast, urban North Central, and Pacific states. The Southeast and West North Central states maintained relatively high dependency ratios throughout the 1950s. Mississippi, New Mexico, and Utah had the highest ratios in both 1950 and 1960.

As child dependency throughout the nation increased, so did expenditures for schooling. Expenditure per pupil in average daily full-time attendance in 1949–50 was $209 for the United States and reached $294 in 1955–56,[7] represent-

[6] See Bernert, *America's Children*, Chapter 3. Educational performance is measured in terms of deviations from an expected age-grade school progress. See also Chapter 6.
[7] U.S. Department of Health, Education, and Welfare. Office of

ing a 40 percent increase over the earlier date. Though proportionate increases were greater in the Southern states, the South still spends considerably less for schooling than states in the other regions. With a third of the nation's children and youth in the Southern states, school expenditures per pupil in average daily attendance in 1955–56 came to only $222 as compared with expenditures in the Northeast, where less than a fourth of the children in the United States reside, of $323 per pupil. About 30 percent of the children live in the North Central States, which expend on the average $304 per pupil attending school. The states of the West, containing less than 15 percent of the children, expend an average of $318 per pupil in average daily attendance.

Mississippi, despite almost doubling its school expenditure between 1949–50 and 1955–56 ($88 per pupil 1949–50 and $157 per pupil 1955–56) still spends considerably less for schooling than any other state. New York, on the other hand, spends more than any other state, reaching $426 per pupil in average daily attendance in 1955–56.

Living and Family Arrangements

Nearly all children in the United States live with one or both parents or other relatives. Of over 60 million children in 1958 about 97 percent were living with one or both parents or other relatives, and about a quarter of a million were living away from relatives, as residents of institutions, as foster children, or as wards.

Education, *Biennial Survey of Education in the United States, 1954–56*, "Statistics of State School Systems," Chapter 2, Table 41.

Most children were living with one or both parents in their own households, though about 2.5 million were with one or both parents who were sharing the living quarters of someone else. Over 90 percent of these children whose parents were sharing living quarters were living in the homes of grandparents or some other relative.

Although the average size of families has not changed significantly since 1950 (3.5 in 1950 and 3.6 in 1958), in the past several years the number of families with two or more children living at home increased more than the number of families with no children or with just one child. In 1958 there were 16.4 million families with two or more of their own children at home—an increase of 5.2 million families or 46 percent over a ten-year period. During this same period the number of families with no children or with only one child showed much less change, 27.3 million in 1958, as compared with 26.1 million in 1948.

The increase in the number of children per family during the past decade or more has been far greater among nonfarm families than among farm families. In 1958, 40 percent of the nonfarm husband-wife families had two or more children living with them. Ten years earlier only 31 percent of these families had two or more children living at home. Comparable figures for farm husband-wife families are 42 percent in 1958 and 40 percent in 1948. These recent gains in the number of children in nonfarm families have almost removed the differences between the two groups of families in this respect.

CHILDREN IN BROKEN FAMILIES. The family as an institution

has changed in many respects in the past several decades, with many of its earlier functions and activities now met by outside agencies. Clothing is usually bought ready-made; there is considerably less food processing in the household; there is considerable commercial recreation outside the home; and into the hands of the school has fallen a variety of educational, disciplinary, health, and socialization functions. However, the family is still regarded as the central mechanism for the transmission of culture, and as the most practical means of caring for children until they can assume their adult responsibilities. Generally, to fulfill this purpose there is a differentiation of roles, or a division of labor, among family members. Typically the father is provider and the mother is homemaker. Circumstances which alter or interfere with the performance of these roles often create problems which threaten the survival of the family itself and give rise to problems of adjustment for the children.

In 1950 there were 4.1 million and in 1958 about 5.6 million children under eighteen years of age, who were not living with both their mother and father; most of these children were living with one parent. These one-parent families, numbering about 3 million in 1958, represent "broken" families and are the result of marital discord and widowhood, as well as service in the armed forces, civilian employment elsewhere, and extended hospitalization. The largest number of children not living with both parents, about 4.7 million, were in families headed by a woman, generally the mother. Separated, widowed, and divorced parents comprise the vast majority of family heads in "broken" homes and a much smaller proportion are parents who are living apart for reasons other than marital discord or military service.[8] A larger proportion of nonfarm families than of farm families are among those which have been disrupted for various reasons.

Women carry the major burden of broken homes, not only because of their longer life span, but also because children usually remain with the mother when a marriage is disrupted by divorce or separation. Furthermore, the evidence suggests that the role of children as deterrents upon family disruption has been steadily weakening. Both the number of broken families and the number of dependent children involved in these families have been rising gradually during the past few decades.[9]

Any break in the home is likely to be a critical experience in the life of the child. In some instances it may draw the remaining members of the family closer together, making for greater integration. However, it is more likely, especially in cases of divorce and separation, to create problems of adjustment for the child and parents, often leading to further disintegration of the family unit, and possibly of the personality of the child. Also, a large proportion of the broken family units are not self-supporting, giving rise to many other derivative problems.

[8] Glick, *American Families*, p. 41, analyzes comparable data for 1953. Of 5.8 million children living with one parent, 1.5 million were living with a separated parent, 1.5 million with a widowed parent, 1.1 million with a divorced parent, .5 million with a mother while father was absent in military service, and 1.1 million were living with one parent while the other was absent from home for reasons other than marital discord or military service. In 1955 there were about 5.8 million children living in "broken families."

[9] Bernert, *America's Children*, pp. 36–39.

Income of Families with Children

Recent estimates of family income levels indicate that median income for all families in 1958 continued its upward trend, although the increase was smaller than previously. The median family income amounted to about $3,100 in 1949, $3,700 in 1951, $4,400 in 1955, $4,800 in 1956, and $5,000 in 1957. Half of the children in the nation (30 million) in 1957 were living in families whose total income was less than $5,000, and 15 to 20 percent of the children (about 11 million) were living in families whose annual income in 1957 was less than $2,500. Over 40 percent of the children in 1957 were living in families whose annual income was $5,000 to $10,000, and about 7 percent were in families earning $10,000 or more.

The weight of cumulative evidence in the past has demonstrated that families with larger numbers of children tend to be in lower income brackets than do those with fewer children. This pattern of differentials is again demonstrated in the data for the past decade. In both 1952 and 1957 the median income of families with one or two children exceeded the median income for all families. The median income among families with four or more children was lower than the median income for all families at both time periods. It is interesting to note, however, that at the latter date the highest median income was achieved in families of three children, while at the earlier date the income of families with three children was about the same as that for all families.

Among families with children in 1958, there was an

average of 2.6 children in families which earned a median income of less than $2,500 as contrasted with 2.1 average number of children in families with $10,000 or more income. Similar figures for 1950 were 2.4 children where the family income was less than $1,000 and 1.9 where the family income was $6,000 or more during the preceding year.

WORKING MOTHERS. The mother often enters the labor market for the purpose of raising the level of family living. In 1958, there were about 6 million families with children under eighteen where both parents were in the labor force. In addition there were almost 1.5 million mothers of dependent children in the labor force who were widowed, divorced, or living apart from their husbands for various reasons. In March, 1958, about 20 percent of the mothers of pre-school age children were in the labor force—following a gradual increase in this proportion from the time of World War II. (The comparable figure in 1950 was less than 15 percent.) Included in this group of 2.85 million working mothers of children under six were 450,000 who were widowed, divorced, or living apart from their husbands for other reasons.

About 40 percent of the mothers of school-age children were in the labor force in 1958, as compared with about 25 percent in 1950. Included in this group of over 4.5 million mothers were about 1 million who were not living with their husbands.

Labor force participation rates were highest for wives without children in the household, intermediate for wives with children six to seventeen years old, and lowest for those with children under six years of age. Also, as the husband's income increased there was a decline in the labor force participation of wives who had children in the household.

Undoubtedly the employment of mothers of young children involves some readjustment in family life patterns, particularly with respect to the care of children. In the spring of 1958 there were about 2 million children under six years of age whose mothers were working full time. The largest proportion of these children—about 40 percent—were being cared for by relatives, other than their parents, including older children, usually siblings. About 20 percent were in the care of their own mothers or fathers who either worked different shifts or who were able to have the children with them at their work. Approximately 25 percent were cared for by neighbors or other nonrelatives. Only 5 percent were placed in care centers such as nursery schools, settlement houses, etc.[10]

There are many aspects of the absence of the mother from the home and such items as time and duration of her employment are of obvious importance. To the extent that the hours and place of employment are adjusted to permit the mother to fulfil her domestic and maternal duties, the effect upon young children may be different from what is usually the case when working hours and place are not adjusted.

[10] Henry C. Lajewski, "Working Mothers and Their Arrangements for Care of Their Children," *Social Security Bulletin* (August, 1959), Vol. 22, No. 8.

Youth at Work

Available data on the labor force participation of youths have shown a rapid decline in rate of participation from the turn of the century to World War II. In contrast to 1900 when almost 45 percent of the youths aged fourteen to nineteen years were in the labor force, in 1940 about one-quarter of the youths were labor force members. By 1950 over a third of those fourteen to nineteen years of age were numbered among the civilian labor force. In 1959 there were still almost 5 million youths aged fourteen to nineteen years in the civilian labor force, representing about a third of the population of these ages. An additional 6 million young persons, twenty to twenty-four years of age, were in the labor force, which at that time totaled about 69 million.

Since the time of World War II the predominant pattern of work for young people of high-school age has been the part-time employment of students. A 1957 survey shows that of 2.7 million youths fourteen to seventeen years of age in the labor force, about 2 million were enrolled in school and most of them were working part time. Among those doing nonagricultural work only a small percentage were employed full time and about two-thirds worked less than fifteen hours per week.

Young workers in recent years, as in previous years, were employed predominantly in industries and occupations which require relatively little skill or previous work experience. Wholesale and retail trades (where young boys are primarily engaged as newsboys and delivery boys) and agriculture (which employs youngsters as farm laborers) account for over two-thirds of the employment of males of high-school ages. Young female workers were employed primarily in the service industries, largely as private household workers; a smaller, though considerable, proportion were employed by retail trade establishments as salesgirls.

In general, changes in the industrial affiliations of young workers were similar to changes in the affiliations of all employed persons. To this extent these changes may be said to reflect shifts in the economic structure of the nation, but the difference in changes which occurred between young workers and total workers may be said to reflect more the variations in the employment opportunities offered to youthful and to mature workers. For example, the teen-age exodus from employment in agriculture has been more pronounced during the past few decades, though agriculture still provides employment for a larger proportion of young people than of total workers. Similarly in retail trade, growth has been more marked in teen-age employment than in total employment. Increases in manufacturing industries, on the other hand, were much greater for the total employed than for the teen-agers.

There are pronounced shifts in the type of work young people do as they advance in age. Among the eighteen- and nineteen-year-old boys, for example, less than 20 percent were employed in agriculture in contrast to those of high-school ages where agriculture accounted for over a third of their total employment (generally as unpaid family workers). Greater employment in manufacturing industries and the trade industries as operators, craftsmen, and clerical workers indicate the increasing responsibility and remuneration achieved by the older boys.

Similarly among the young women clerical jobs in manufacturing and trade and service work other than in private households predominate among the eighteen- and nineteen-year-olds, whereas domestic and retail sales work provide the largest share of employment among the younger girls.

In July, 1957, a special inquiry was made on the summer work activity among children ten to thirteen years of age—who normally are not covered in labor force figures. Of the 12 million children of these ages at that time about 1.8 million or 15 percent were doing some kind of work. This compares with 1.1 million children (12 percent) of the same ages similarly employed in the summer of 1950. At both periods young boys comprised the bulk of this child-worker group—about 70 percent of the total. In 1950 17 percent of these young boys were working. In 1957 the proportion of working boys increased to 21 percent. The percentage of working girls increased from 7 to 9 percent between the two dates.

Though there are considerably more white children engaged in some kind of work activity (over 85 percent of the total) the proportion of nonwhite girls who were working was almost double that of white girls. Among boys the proportion was about the same.

About a million children, or 55 percent of the ten- to thirteen-year-olds who work, work as farm laborers—more than half of whom were family workers. Most of the others were employed as newsboys, laborers, and private household workers (probably on odd-jobs, or as babysitters).

The hours of work reported by these youngsters were considerably shorter than those for workers of high-school age. It also appears that the work weeks were shorter for the ten- to thirteen-year-olds in 1957 than in 1950. Almost 80 percent of the youngsters working in nonagricultural endeavors reported a work week of less than fifteen hours and all but about 5 percent of them worked less than thirty-five hours a week.

When children of these ages are working on farms, however, especially as unpaid family workers, they put in considerably longer hours on the job. Over a third of the youngsters on farms worked thirty-five or more hours a week.

Summary and Conclusions

The rise in the numbers of children and youth in the United States which began during World War II continued during the decade of the '50s, although it leveled off among those under five years of age. Coupling this growth in the actual numbers of children and youth with continuous improvement in school enrollment rates (already maximized in the compulsory school ages and rising among the pre- and post-compulsory school ages) gives rise to one of the most pressing concerns today—the provision of adequate educational facilities. Within the next five years our elementary schools will be faced with enrollments of 34 to 35 million children; by 1970, this figure may reach 37 to 40 million children. High schools will greet some 13 million youths in 1965 and about 14 million in 1970. An additional 2.5 to 3 million youths eighteen and nineteen years old may be enrolling in schools in 1965 and later. Potential students among those aged twenty to thirty-four years will add more than another 2.5 to 3 million students during the years ahead.

To further complicate the issue of providing adequate educational and other facilities for the swelling numbers of children and youth is the concomitant decline in the proportion of population in the productive ages, the group whose efforts usually provide the support for these services and facilities. Ten years ago there were about two persons of productive ages for each child under eighteen years of age. Today there are only 1.5 persons of productive age for each child. With a decline in the ratio of producers per dependent, the population may find it increasingly difficult to provide the required services for both the child and aged dependents.

The balance between the dependent and productive age groups continues to favor urban areas over rural and farm areas. And the balance remains most favorable in those states where economic resources are greater. In those states where economic resources basic to the provision of facilities for dependent groups are relatively low, the dependency ratios are high. The South, which produces over a third of the nation's children and youth, has the least favorable child dependent-producer ratio, relatively low average family income, low expenditures for schooling, low educational attainment among adults, and relatively poor educational performance among school children. Large numbers of migrants leave the South for the North and West. The segregated social environment of white and Negro children in the South also has significant effects on the adequacy of the training for adulthood which is provided in these states.

Most children in the United States live with one or both parents or other relatives. There has been an increase, however, in the number of children living in broken families caused primarily by marital discord or widowhood. Women continue to bear the major burden of broken homes.

The income of families having children has risen gradually over the past several decades, as has the total income of all families in the United States. However, there are over 10 million children in the country today who live in families whose income is grossly inadequate for the provision of even minimum opportunities for growth and development. It is these children particularly, whose families earn less than $2,500 a year, who need special services.

The number of children with working mothers has also been increasing in the past decade. Although a recent survey shows that most of these children who are of preschool age are being cared for by relatives or neighbors, the quality and nature of this mother-surrogate care might well be assessed along with the possible use and services provided by professional care centers.

From the early days of social enlightenment there has been much talk and concern about youngsters being put to work. The activities of several generations of interested persons and agencies coupled with the maturation of our modern industrial life have resulted in effective child labor laws, compulsory school regulations, and attitudes generally favorable to a minimization of child labor. The employment of youngsters ten to thirteen years old is now largely confined to family farms, paper routes, and babysitting or household chores.

Among the youths of high-school age the predominant pattern of work has been the part-time employment of students—combining the advantages of continued schooling with an early and gradual introduction into the adult world. Among the older youths, between eighteen and twenty-four years of age, full-time employment is, of course, more common than is the combination of school and work. However, school enrollment rates among these age groups have increased considerably, suggesting marked improvement in the holding power of our schools beyond the compulsory attendance ages.

Much attention has been paid of late to the numbers of young people, still largely economically dependent, who are being married. Though the number and percentage of married teen-agers increased markedly during the late 1940s and early '50s, a review of the data indicates that there has been little change since the early 1950s. In 1950 1.1 million teenagers or 9 percent were married as compared with 1.5 million or 8 percent in 1958. To the extent that marriage disrupts the continued schooling of these youths, sending them into the labor market prematurely, a penalty is paid in the form of lost opportunities for economic, cultural, and personal advancement. To the extent that parental attitudes and resources as well as increased employment opportunities for student-workers encourage these youths to complete their education, it is conceivable that early marriage and family formation may reap the advantages of providing alternative pathways to adult life. Here is an area about which little is known and one which is ripe for future investigation.

THE AMERICAN FAMILY IN THE PERSPECTIVE OF OTHER CULTURES

by CONRAD M. ARENSBERG

THAT the family is part of the universal experience of mankind we know to be true. It is also true, however, that the family experience of the modern United States has very special features. In considering American families and their effect upon children at home and in society, it is necessary to be clear as to universal characteristics of the American family and as to its special or unique features.

In part, of course, the special features of the American family, in comparison with the family of other parts of the world, are twentieth-century products. In far greater part, however, they are enduring particularities of American culture, built upon American inheritances from Europe. This specificity of the cultural tradition which has shaped the American culture and its characteristic family life is quite striking when we match American family experience against that of most of the extra-European world of both today and yesterday. The family traditions of Europe, like other aspects

Conrad M. Arensberg is Professor of Anthropology at Columbia University.

of European civilization, have been reworked and reshaped here, rather than those of Asian, African, or other civilizations, in the succeeding stages of our national development and amalgamation. Much American custom, modern and self-evident as it may seem to us, is both unique in the world and old and special in kind because it happened to have the particular special European beginnings on which it was built.

In world perspective, then, we must first note that the American family, seen generally, shares many aspects of family life and organization, first of all and very deeply, with Great Britain and the other European countries, particularly the northern and western ones. Some of these European roots are very ancient. The United States has been and is still a great mixture of peoples and conditions. Seen comparatively, its culture is new, recently unified from an assemblage of diverse regions, classes, and ethnic groups. Majority and minority ethnic strains, yielding American subcultures, have evolved an American family life, perhaps not yet completely unified but making a fairly well-understood common ideal pattern which continues to show variations dependent upon different social traditions and different past and present circumstances of economic, religious, and social life.

The common or generally perceived ideal pattern of family life in the United States today shapes our formal institutions and our legal system, lends its values to popular culture and public education, and influences strongly many of the national characteristics of our people. Nevertheless, in dealing realistically with problems of intercultural and intergroup contact and understanding, with difficulties over juvenile delinquency, with the responsibilities of social work, public and private, one must also recognize and cope with many deviations from this general majority culture pattern, anchored in the variant ethnic, regional, and class traditions and circumstances. In discussing the American family as it compares with those of other lands and civilizations both the general pattern and the exceptions to it must be presented.

To put the American family and its variants in proper perspective, then, there are two possible courses. One is to discuss the historical factors that have been at work to produce American civilization in general and lay before the reader their influence upon the family within that civilization. But such a task is better left to the historian. Another course is to outline the kinds and varieties of family organization and experience which anthropological science has revealed in its study of comparative social structure among all human cultures both primitive and civilized, in all epochs and on all the continents, and then to place the American ways with family life in their right place among these.

Our present paper will take the second course. The highly particular, in some ways unique, features of American family life come to the fore better in such a presentation, where contrasts between the familiar and the unfamiliar customs of mankind help the reader see his own American way in sharper outline. In such contrasts well-known facts of American historical development take on added meaning when they are seen operating against the different traditions still continuing in the world outside of Europe but nevertheless in essential continuation of the original and specially European cultural and familial traditions which gave them their beginnings. In taking the world-wide, fully anthropological perspective, we can trace the American family's evolution to its own maturity from its European origins and see more fully the cultural continuities involved. We can avoid thus the temptation to think of our own American family experience as much like others in kind but somehow different chiefly because it is luckier, more progressive, and more modern than that of the rest of mankind. Modern anthropological science, indeed, has come to reveal how very rich, complex, and diverse have been the differing forms of family life and organization of human beings round the world, in cultures both primitive and civilized. This complexity and diversity, indeed, continues to exist even in the "one world" of modern communication. The perspective of this revelation is necessary if we are to see American family life as others must see it from Asia, from Africa, from Oceania, even from Europe itself.

In comparing the families of the cultures of the world, it is possible to distinguish between the immediate family and household, surrounding children from their births through their maturation and until they establish families of their own, on the one hand, and the larger "kinship system," uniting immediate families in larger, extended relationships and groupings, on the other. This "kinship system," as the anthropologists call the circle of relatives about each person, obviously unites families across the generations and through marriages, weaving a network of associations and obligations, perhaps even forming a community of succor, cooperation, or defense among the relatives of his own and of his spouse which nearly every man possesses.

The Immediate Household

It is, of course, the universal experience of mankind, in every culture, that a person has a family in which he is born and grows up, providing him for good or ill with a father, a mother, perhaps with brothers and sisters. If this group of parents and siblings fails to exist, we of course take special note that the man is an orphan or product of a "broken" family, an unusual, fateful case. It is equally universal that many if not most of the adults, but not all, in a society, whether primitive tribe or modern civilization, come to head similar families in which they in their turn are parents of children of their own and thus create the next generation. The two families most persons experience have been aptly called the family of orientation (the one in which a person grows up and is oriented toward his world), and the family of procreation (the one in which he is a parent in his turn). The names, naturally, reflect subjective experience; seen more objectively the two families are merely two in a repetitive succession of like social organisms, families, endlessly transmitting cultural and social experience.

Cultural anthropology has gathered up good evidence of the universal occurrence of these elementary human groupings in all the cultures of mankind, past and present. Yet they are not always alike. It is difficult to believe the evidence that has now been amassed as to how various, underneath this universality, the particularities of organization and experience are from country to country and culture to culture and how special is modern American experience. Roles of the sexes, duties of parents, definitions of father, mother, brother, sister, sizes of the household, durations of the obligations and the affections, longevity of the family grouping, any and all of the behaviors, attitudes, and relationships so universal to human experience leave us little more certainty than that some kind of family life is to be counted on in every human community. The details telling us what kind are much more variable than we expect them to be.

The Kinship System

Equally universal is the existence of some sort of kinship system, as we have called the circle of relatives beyond the immediate family. In normal social life—apart from the accidents of orphanhood, the breaking up of families by emigration or discord or the decimations of population brought by war, famine, or pestilence; and also apart from the special individualizing changes of modern life such as rapid and impersonal urbanizations and industrializations—most of mankind have been and still are born into a web of relationships uniting other families to their own. Through their parents they are brought into a circle of secondary relatives large or small, alive or dead but remembered, giving them their grandparents, uncles, aunts, cousins, and so on, like the ones "reckoned up by dozens" in the song of Gilbert and Sullivan. Later on most persons who marry spouses not orphans or isolates acquire upon marrying another such circle or "family" of inlaws, technically called affinal relatives, as opposed to the first set, their "blood" kin or consanguinal relatives, now relatives who are in turn relatives of their children.

The existence of both types of relatives, consanguinal and affinal, still "family" in the larger sense of relationships of familial and kinship sort, is another universal of human culture. Groupings of such sort mark the social organization and the customary moralities of every culture and society and always have. Their weakening, their disappearance, or their supplantation or disestablishment by the state or by individualism is a matter of interest and comment to social scientists, and it is only recently in political evolution that law and civil right have come to strip them of legal and political force over individuals as in our modern civil codes. Here again, if modern conditions seem to have diminished the importance of such kindreds for Americans, to the point where American discussion of the family tends to omit them altogether, and if modern life seems sometimes to weaken the customs of kinship obligation and responsibility almost to nothing, and even to increase markedly the number of persons in society who are without such relatives or think themselves free of them, then these facts of change away from the usual expectancies of human social life are unusual and deserve special comment.

Today social scientists, moralists, reformers, social workers, and persons concerned with the welfare of dependent persons, old people, women, as well as children, all note alike the decay of kinship in modern life. They all alike note the growing isolation of the immediate family and the small household, not only from ties of neighborhood and residential community but also from those of kinship with other families, from parents and relatives of any sort. The decay of kinship ties is not always regretted. It seems to have been specially marked under American historical conditions calling for great mobility, for free movement from place to place, occupation to occupation, the prerequisites of an "open" society such as ours. American moral and ethical imperatives of personal and small-family self-reliance seem also to have supported the man who could "go it alone," "make a fresh start," "make his own way," free of entangling kindred. But here again the special American accent on kinship does not exempt American family experience from participation in the universality of kinship organization in human cultures; it merely shows us the radical character of the American treatment of kindreds.

Here again, however, the universality of some type of kinship extending beyond the immediate family is merely the first comparative fact we must note. The types of kinship system and the groupings, obligations, the moral imperatives upon persons, the reliances and entanglements to which they put most people in the many and varied societies of the world, past and present, are unbelievably varied and differing. Modern anthropological science has revealed, here too, how strong and ruling kinship customs still are in the world of today, and how various they continue to be in their not yet relaxed hold upon the nationals of country after country in the world nowadays, not only in the underdeveloped areas

where premodern conditions still persist but into the upper
ranks of civilized persons everywhere, despite the attacks of
every kind of modern doctrine, from Communism to democratic idealism, upon such remnants of a pre-individualist
order. Anthropology can place modern American custom
quite precisely in its likeness and unlikeness to kinship systems in other countries and continents, and is beginning to
understand better the effects upon psychology and upon welfare of the especial decay of the institution in our land. Here,
too, once more, both the remarkable diversity of custom
extant in the world and the special character of the European
beginnings upon which American kinship has been built will
probably surprise us.

The Institution of Marriage

Another universal of human organization we must mention
in order to place the American family in proper comparative
perspective is the existence of some sort of marriage in every
recorded human society. Every culture anthropology has
studied carries some sort of customary legal or moral sanction
upon the recognized near-exclusive association of particular
male and female human beings. Usually but not necessarily
always these are mates, partners in the procreating of and the
caring for the children of an immediate household or small
family. Thus, we can speak of a "biological" family man
shares in some ways even with the higher animals. This serves
to unite sex partners at least for the years when children require care and extends sexual association into parental association and cooperation.

But here again we must be careful not to mistake American custom and morality for universalities of human experience and social organization. In many cultures and civilizations the conjugal relation and the cooperation of married partners may well not be the central family relationship at all. Filial and fraternal relationships may be stronger; grandmothers and aunts may have more to do with bringing up children than mothers; mothers' brothers, not fathers, may discipline children, transmit inheritances, represent the family before the community, etc. The immediate equation we make between a married couple and a family, when we think instinctively of the family as a small group dominated by immediate parents of minor children, betrays us into error. Especially, our notion that each married couple lives by itself and by itself constitutes a family, so that we can even speak of a childless married pair as a "family without children" or call a wife or a husband "my family," fails us in many parts even of the modern world.

The anthropological facts are simply that marriages and families always exist, but they differ from ours quite often and interconnect in different ways from ours. While all cultures show some sort of marriage, in the sense of a sanctioned preferential right of association, sexual, economic, proprietary, between one or more men and one or more women, in many parts of the world still today and in many civilizations in history marital unions have not necessarily been nor are they now monogamous, nor even theoretically permanent, nor need husband and wife always live together, nor do necessarily they "cleave together and forsake all others," nor

need they be the main source of either their own livelihood
or the care, protection, discipline, and legal identification of
their children. Other family systems than ours can and do
assign all these functions to other relatives and groupings of
relatives than the father and mother as husband and wife in
a small family. Our American assumptions, equating marrying, setting up an independent household, and supporting a
spouse and children as coincident responsibilities of a family
life, take our custom for granted and mistake it for an inevitable and universal fact of human life. But once again we
must see American family experience, particularly where it
makes a successful marital partnership a principal, if not the
sole source of love and security for children and of happiness
and self-esteem for adults, as in some ways a special product
of a highly particular and limited European and American
social and legal evolution.

Indeed, in some ways our equation of family stability and
successful marital partnership, which American ideals urge
upon us, is almost a world extreme both in the reduction of
the family in size as a social unit and in central emphasis
upon the conjugal tie, with its interspouse adjustment and
cooperation, as a basis for family living. Our democratic and
individualist traditions and our feminine revolution have
brought us costs as well as victories. The imperatives of our
family system, basing the small household on the conjugal
pair, isolating that pair to free them to command their own
destinies and satisfactions and to confer on them nearly complete and untrammeled authority over minor children (ex-

cept where the state and community limit them), are not easy ones. Nor is the task our educational ideal assumes a simple one: to prepare each and every man and woman to be in adulthood spouse, parent, householder, and family head all at once. These imperatives of our present small, conjugal type of family, with its minimum of kinship entanglement and support, ideally require each person to find a mate for himself, to love that spouse, to share the upbringing of children with him or her, to maintain a household with him, to find chief emotional identification in the little family growing up around this spouse and partner freely chosen and freely retained. To carry all these roles is not easy and to put so many eggs in one basket is certainly risky; few other family customs or national cultures seem to require such concentration of emotional effort in individual responsibility for self-directed personal adjustment and for unaided child-training. Here again, American family custom has special features, imperatives, and problems, arising out of a special past and responding, perhaps, to special present conditions.

These, then, are the universalities. Families, marital unions, kinship systems are present in every human society and culture. But they are shaped differently; they interconnect in many various ways; they assume different relative importances in the functions of support of every kind, from livelihood to affection, they perform for human beings, both the grown-up ones and the children. Let us see more closely where American family, marriage, and kinship, with their special American interconnections, fit in.

The Middle-Class Ideal

First, the American family is distinguished by the great importance, emphasis upon, and independence of the small, immediate or "biological" family of father and mother and minor children. American custom attempts to generalize this small unit, free it, trains most persons for roles heading it in adult life, delegates societal and legal authority over and responsibility for children almost exclusively to immediate parents in it. In spite of some recent increases in the birth rate this unit is small; on an average households are four and five persons at most; they begin with a marriage of two potential parents, the spouses, who are urged to take up residence, ideally, by themselves and away from others, "undoubling" the larger households of larger, three-generation families still common in many of our recent European immigrant and even our Southern populations; they swell for some years while minor children appear and grow to young adulthood; they contract thereafter as children leave for an existence and a family life of their own.

The unit is not only small, so that households are small and mobile, the family following the husband as he moves from job to job, position to position, or town to town, increasing its isolation not only from kindred but from neighbors and fellows of the community, in the great fluidity of American occupational and residential life, but it is often very short-lived. Not only are divorces common, contributing the major cause of family dissolution (rather than war deaths or famine or emigration of husbands, as in less fortunate countries) but the termination of family life in a period of "the empty nest," with the spouses returned to a life together without children, is a standard, approved, and even planned-for regularity of American social life. Just as the children are trained for the day when they will "leave home" and "have a family of their own," so old people are (ideally) expected to live apart and alone, visited perhaps by adult children but not sharing a household with them, an eventuality perfectly natural in most parts of the world, where gaffers and dowagers may even rule the roost and certainly more often continue in it than leave it as here. But here even the small family endures, in an American's life time, only twenty years or so, especially when the parents ideally have all their children in their younger married years.

All this custom, most of it ideal middle-class American family life whose real prevalence in our mixed and varied population we can only guess at, reflects, obviously, the individual and equalitarian ideals of our country's social and political life, the spread of a wage-earning and money-and-credit consuming way of economic life among most of our people as well as the already mentioned traditional cultural emphasis upon the small family, with its connections to the free choice of mate and residence and occupation and to the open mobility between places and statuses of our society. All those things, together with the reduction of extended family relationships of kinship, inherent in the freeing of individuals from fixed and hereditary placements and categorizations, have marked our civilization since the overthrow of the "ancien régime." We have already cited the historical influences. But the special traditional cultural descent of this kind of family custom which present American conditions continue to deepen and generalize should be noted as well.

The Joint-Family

The best anthropological classification of the families of mankind treats them first as they vary in progressive size of the family unit, particularly as that unit forms the usual households of a society. Largest are the joint-families of India, the patriarchal families of the Chinese gentry of yesterday, the large households of the Middle Eastern countries, of much of Africa where they may be also polygynous, the *zadrugas* and other patriarchal households of the peasant lands which in the the remote Balkans still today practice a household economy like that of ancient Rome. Here a founder, his sons, his sons' sons and all their wives, children, grandchildren, dependents and servants or slaves live their lives out in a house or compound of many rooms with common fields, gardens, and larder under central authority and in common defense for a lifetime. Eventually such a family usually splits to make more like it; the common lands or joint economy make greater size of household equivalent to strength and security; and the continually splitting households often retain ties of common defense, including even blood vengeance, to form far-flung clans of common unilineal descent.

We tend to forget how widespread even today, especially in the underdeveloped countries, are such great families and how common such clans, with the security and the trammels they bring, still are in the world. Because we have forgotten them, or belong to traditions which never knew them, does not mean they are any the less viable alternate ways of organizing individual and community life, imposing imperatives, and requiring virtues of their own kind, in many parts of the world where the national state is still new and where kinsmen and patrons rather than the national police protect individuals. In such lands they are still to be found, still opposing or braking the individualizing forces of modern pecuniary economics and of modern civil law. Some of our American ethnic groups, both immigrant and native, have strong and recent memories of joint households and clan ties, so different from the individuation of the small family of our majority tradition. When their households, for example, give over child care to grandmothers or take in nephews and cousins on the same basis as immediate children, sometimes in direct clash with our family law and our welfare procedures based on our small-family custom in which such relatives have no claim or right of care and protection, the difference in custom and family organization goes unacknowledged and the clash between public procedures and private interests and capabilities unresolved.

The Stem-Family

Our small-family tradition is based, of course, on quite other cultural antecedents than the joint-family and the clan uniting forever all the sons and grandsons of so-and-so. The next classification of families and households common in many parts of the world bases them on a size intermediate between the great households of the joint families and our own small ones. American experience, indeed American social science, does not recognize this classification and fails to note that it is very widespread in the world, particularly in Europe, but also in Asian peasant lands, especially where small proprietorship has fostered the growth and transmission of inherited family farms. In the European countries, especially in those of small peasant holdings, France, Germany, Ireland, northern Italy and northern Spain, etc., but also in Japan, the Philippines (Ifugao, for instance) and in parts of peasant India and China both, an intermediate size of family and household, living for generation after generation on a family holding, has often become standard and customary. This counted in the homestead in each generation the peasant holder, his wife, his minor children, his unmarried brothers or sisters, living as unpaid farm laborers and helping him until they should move away or marry off, his father and mother, perhaps retired from active work but still influential and assisting. If one of the standard disasters of peasant subsistence agriculture was to be avoided, namely the endless equal subdivision of the plot among children until no one child inherited land enough for subsistence, then in each generation the family homestead and plot should be kept intact and undivided. One child, or at most two, should be heirs of the whole, becoming the new holder in turn, and his noninheriting brothers and sisters should have to find for themselves some other provision in life than a bit of the family lands or else remain at home forever in a minor, farm-helper status.

Through matchmaking and other mechanisms such restriction of inheritance to a single heir in each generation often became standard, acceptable, even ideal. The household and lands remained a stem or source of new heirs and new emigrants in each successive generation; a long line of holders kept the homestead in the line or stem; it even, usually, carried the name of the farm as a family name. Each generation knew a three-generation household of retired parents, heir and his spouse (either a son or a daughter might get the land as heir of the intact holding and Norman-French primogeniture and estate entail was merely one version of such custom). Each generation knew new waves of brothers and sisters, noninheriting children who must go out into the world to "make their fortunes" elsewhere, on new farms, in marriages outside, in the apprenticeships leading to artisan or other work in the cities.

This kind of family organization became and is still standard in most of the European countries, whence its name coined by the great French family sociologist LePlay comes: the *famille-souche* or the stem-family (*Stammfamilie*, in German). It seems historically in Europe to have grown up with the medieval transition between tribal landholding and peasant tenancy and proprietorship.

So deeply is it ingrained in European tradition, whether peasant or of higher class, that many discussions between Anglo-Saxons and Europeans founder on the unrecognized adherence of Anglo-Saxon tradition to the small-family and the usual European to the stem-family. Where an American, and an Englishman, in the small-family tradition, may

be enjoined by his own desires, his wife, and his columnist
of manners and personal problems, such as a Mary Hay-
worth, to set his old mother up to live alone and think it
a hardship to have her under the same roof with his wife
and children, a Frenchman may define the *foyer* (intimate
family) to include her and regard it as unthinkable that
grand'mère live anywhere else. Much of the "Americaniza-
tion" of modern Americans involves undoubling of such
stem-family households today, the dissolution of family kit-
ties which pool the incomes and the salaries of even adult
children, a usual and expectable European practice in many
countries—indeed even necessary where "family allowances"
and state pensions do not even presume individual wage
equalities or reckon a living wage to include a family livelihood as with us. Countless thousands of Americans of
second-generation or third-generation immigrant origin or
even of American Southern and Southern Hill background
are new and transitional to the small-family, individualizing
family tradition, moving toward it from the other moralities
of the stem-family tradition, in a way analogous to that in
which we can today find Yugoslavia moving from joint-
family (*zadruga*) to stem-family (European peasant) organization with attendant difficulties of social change and adjustment. Our social sciences are still too young to let us
know and recognize the many modern cultural and social
transitions of this kind and to let us deal adequately with
their personal and psychological costs. Only in recent years
have the social work and welfare professions begun to recognize such transitions and to learn that caseworkers must be

prepared to face them. Public and legal recognition of private customary differences of family interests and definitions is, indeed, not yet in sight.

Family Transformations

The general European movement of family organization during the Middle Ages seems to have been much that of Yugoslavia in recent decades, a movement from joint-family and clan protection for individuals and great-household economy, even for peasants, to smaller peasant subsistence holdings, of stem-family kind, with proprietorship passed down the line of family heirs. There is reason to believe that some parts of Europe, like some parts of the non-European world, never took part in this transition, chiefly because, as we shall see, small families and weak kinship units were aboriginal, part of another way of life than peasant subsistence. Deferring that suggestion for a moment, let us see what kind of kinship evolution took place as stem-families, if not conjugal small ones like ours, succeeded, at least in Europe, joint-families and great-households.

One change was certainly the spread of bilateral as opposed to unilateral kinship units, a shift from exclusive clans of the kind we have mentioned, to diffuse and general kindreds of the sort we know today, in which all the blood descendants of the same grandparents and great-grandparents as our own, are our cousins, regardless of whether they come through the male or through the female lines. We still reckon as relatives upon whom we have some claim, if only a bed in emergencies, the whole diffuse circle of such natural

kin; no longer can the world be divided into the sons of my
fathers, whom I must defend to the death, and the sons of
my mother's clan, who may have to shoot me on sight. Only
the family name still, with us as with other Europeans,
descends down the paternal line, as a vague identifier. We
can trace through European history, as we can trace it still
in the spread of the national state today, the shift over to
such stem-names, giving each man a family name. The custom reached Turkey only with Kemal Atatürk's reforms,
and has yet to reach either Indonesia or (oddly enough)
Iceland. We can likewise trace the dissolution of clans and
phratries, still alive in Arabia or Pakistan, with the shift to
the kind of bilateral, diffuse, cousin-counting kinship we ourselves know. In this shift to diffuse, relative reckoning of
significant kinship, from a former counting instead of exclusive and corporate groups of special legal and moral force,
we can still see a background to the individuation and the
liberation from status and adherence prescribed at birth
that has gone so far, as we have pointed out, in our own
American treatment of kinship.

Let us at last return to that part of the European tradition
in which, as with our own Anglo-Saxon heritage, neither the
stem-family of the peasantries nor the fixities of joint-family
and clan figured. Other parts of the world, as we said,
have been found by social anthropologists to possess small-
family organization. Notably these are some of the hunting
peoples organized for a subsistence requiring great movement
and fluidity among small bands of persons and, oddly enough,
many of the civilized peoples of South East Asia; Malays,

Thai, Burmese, etc. There is some evidence, too, that in periods of rapid urbanization, as in ancient Roman days, great movement and migration of persons and extreme fluidity of occupational life and easy social mobility have tended more than once to dissolve kinship rigidities, to isolate and free individuals and generalize small families, just as in recent British and American history.

A great argument of social science can be waged today whether pecuniary civilization, industrialization, the factory system in themselves do not force a generalization of small families, and indeed the European practice is to treat the small family, which we call the "democratic" type of family organization, as the "proletarian" or the "disorganized" one. But the argument is better left to one side, the more so as Japan, India, the Middle East, and even such countries as Belgium and Germany seem to be able to undergo industrialization without a wholesale or even a widespread adoption of American and British small-family social patterns. The only causative argument or association we can advance for the distribution in the world of small families as the standard family system of a culture is that any pattern of economic subsistence requiring fluid movement of persons and alternate sources of hands for impermanent productive units, whether bands of gatherers or hunters, or crews of fishing boats, or short-lived reindeer herds, or new factories recruiting temporary labor forces, seems to favor small-family generalization.

The historical dominance of small-family organization in Great Britain and the nearer parts of North Europe is another problem, not at all to be solved by reference to the Industrial Revolution. The villages of North Europe and of Britain, under the manorial system, seem to have known both stem-families and small-families, and the precarious conditions of medieval farming, with their requirements that a fluid, quickly formed plowteam be formed from any and all neighbors, whether kinsmen or no, at the end of the winters in which only a few oxen or plow-cattle survive to plow the next spring, may well be thought of as favoring the small-family, unobligated peasant, ready to turn to a chance neighbor in the village as quickly as to a cousin or clansman. Certainly by the time the Enclosure Acts had cleared the English villages, destroyed the yeomen who might have duplicated the Grossbauer (big, homesteading peasant) of the continent, and sent out the Puritans and other Dissenters into town life and overseas colonization, the English tradition of small-family life, the generalization of independent starts for children, and the whole apparatus of our modern family system seem already to have been well established.

Our own frontier seems to have spread the Scots-Irish, Southern-Appalachian stem-family tradition. But it also served to spread the Anglo-Saxon, post-medieval, and Puritan small-family way as it spread the English tongue. The Middle West combined and generalized the regional-sectional traditions of our earlier colonial times. Sociologists could note, as late as 1925, that homesteading in Iowa in the sense that farms went to heirs and stayed on with the family line—a definition of the term that stresses holding

on to a farm rather than originally "nesting" it—was confined to German and Polish and Czech Americans. The Old
Americans, "Anglo-Saxons," in that state as elsewhere pre-
ferred to start all the children alike and "independently,"
setting a boy upon the "agricultural ladder," helping him
"start on his own," eventually selling out and dividing the
money equally among all the children, moving on to the West
or to an old age in which the family was dissolved and the
retired farmer and his wife lived apart. The average period
of a farm's stay in one owner's hands became twenty-five
years, the exact duration indeed of a small-family's life, from
the time the young tenant managed (or was helped) to buy
his own farm (if only from father) to the time that he in
his turn retired, sold, and divided the money equally among
his heirs.

The Iowan procedure we are describing here is an excellent example of the American small-family way, with its independent, self-reliant children, all equally on their own, in
contrast to the European *famille-souche*: the peasant household forever in the family line, in which a grown man
is still a boy, still under the family council headed by his
mother and his father, pooling the family's resources, arranging match and dowry for him and sister to the end of
the old people's lives. The attendant dissolution of kinship,
in which a neighbor or fellow-community member is oftener
to be relied on than a cousin, let alone a now nonexistent
clansman, is just another step in the reduction of household
and family size, in the concentration of roles on small-family

personnel, and in the sweeping away of intermediate supports or obligations between the small-family on the one
hand and the community and state on the other.

The particular North European and British, even village
and Puritan English, descent of the American small-family
system is thus quite fateful in the especial evolution of our
family system and its values. The special features of American family experience we noted earlier have legitimate origins in the cultural history of the country as well as in the
special economic, legal, and political historical conditions of
the country's growth. These special features pose special
problems, psychological or other, for Americans. They pose
such problems for Americans both in their own persons as
sharers and movers of the American customs of family life
and in their special difficulties of child welfare and child care.
Many of these latter problems we have already cited: the
isolation of the small family; the brittle dependence for
physical and emotional security, as well as home training and
discipline, upon the competence, cooperation, and adjustment of the spouses; the great and growing age separation
segregating old people and their experience out of family
and even occupational life; the unacknowledged transitions
and exceptions from the ideal small-family morality of the
majority, middle-class, and institutionally-official traditions,
with their conflicts for individuals torn between values taught
at home and values taught in school and community. Most
recent indeed is the continuing weakening of what parental
authority still remains in the parent-spouses, in the spread of
permissive and "democratic" doctrines of family consultation

and enlistment of child interests and prejudices. The father who is not so much a man, a model of adult manhood for his son, as a "pal" and another boy, absent and out of sight in the important, nonfamilial roles of his work existence, has already worried psychiatrists, especially in our newer, dormitory metropolitan suburbs, with their enforced segregation of women and children of limited like age and interests.

Most of these problems, social, legal, and psychological, seem to flow from the continuing evolution of our particular traditions, with the attendant individuation and dissolution of stabilizing and assisting personal contacts in our lives and their replacement by professional and community services. The trend is one that our long evolution of small-family independence and diffusion of kinship and other fixed-status ties long ago began. It is certainly irreversible, even if we wished to reverse it, which our people do not seem to wish to do. But if some information about its special historical character, its special place in the alternate ways of family and community organization in the history of mankind, and its special demands upon ourselves can help us manage better the trends and currents of social change in which we are caught, then perhaps this brief summary of the place of American family life in the perspective of other cultures will have served a purpose.

THE AMERICAN FAMILY TODAY

by REUBEN HILL

AT THE TURN of the century, most people had the greatest respect for the institution called the family, yet they were loath to learn much about it. The family was taken for granted, ignored, shunted aside, and expected to do the nation's patching and mending without reward or attention. According to the cherished beliefs of the period, all husbands and wives lived together in perfect amity and all children loved their parents, to whom they were indebted for the gift of life. Moreover, even if one knew that these things were not true, he ought not to mention it!

Today much of that has been changed. Gone is the concealment of the way in which life begins, gone the irrational sanctity of the home. The aura of sentiment which once protected the family from discussion clings to it no more. It is no longer considered a virtue to be naive or ignorant about the family. We want to learn as much about it as we can and to understand it as thoroughly as possible, for there is a rising recognition in America that vast numbers of its fam-

Reuben Hill is Director of the Minnesota Family Study Center and Professor of Sociology at the University of Minnesota.

ilies are in trouble—sick from internal frustrations and from external pressures in a society which expects the individual family to act as buffer between a poorly integrated social order and the country's children. If fiscal policies are bungled and inflation results, the family purse strings are tightened; if real estate and building interests fail to provide housing, families must adapt themselves to obsolete dwellings or be shoehorned into quarters shared with other families.

The now famous Bill of Rights for Children of the 1930 White House Conference would be no more than a list of platitudes if individual families did not secure these rights for their children. Alas, this is too much to expect of economically and educationally marginal families. This is one reason subsequent White House Conferences have included analysis of the optimum relationship between the family and government and between the family and community planning. We are engaged in the process of reconstructing our family institutions in these conferences through criticism and discussion.

As the ban on discussion of the family has been lifted many have assumed expertness in diagnosing the American family's ills—and their approach usually begins "What's Wrong with the Family?" A wide variety of writers have addressed themselves to this theme recently, and the range of national magazines carrying their articles suggests the high readership provoked by problems of courtship, marriage, and the family. *Life, Look, McCall's, Ladies Home Journal, Better Homes and Gardens, Harper's,* and *The Atlantic* have featured the family and its problems in recent months. College presidents, psychiatrists, ministers, social workers, and judges appear frequently, but included among the authors can be found a labor leader, a motion picture arbiter, an anthropologist, a political commentator, and the American Mother of the Year. Each touches the ailing body of the American family in a different place, but all agree she is ailing. They point to the high divorce rate, to the changes in our sex morality, to juvenile delinquency, and to the rise in forced marriages of teenagers as proof of the breakdown of the family. The causes they list are most varied:

It's the breakdown of character.

It's modern women—they ought to stay home and take care of their children.

It's the search for happiness—we need to return to the old-fashioned virtues of responsibility and adherence to duty.

Alcohol is the key to it all.

There aren't enough parks and playgrounds.

It's poor sex adjustment—what people need are the facts of life.

The trouble is easy divorce—people know they can get out of marriage if it doesn't work.

It's dissimilarity of family backgrounds and temperament.

I regard much of this hue and cry in the public press as useful and healthy, but I do not have too much confidence in the diagnoses advanced by America's self-styled family experts. My approach is that of a family sociologist who has been greatly impressed by the universality of the family as an institution in all countries and in all times, and by its great capacity for adaptation and survival. The social scientist studying the family takes the comparative approach and asks what troubles experienced by the American family are also reported for families in industrializing and urbanizing societies in other parts of the world. From this vantage point it is possible to conclude that many of the disorders of the American family appear to be "growing pains," discomforts incident to adaptive change, normal symptoms of reorganization following adjustment to a new and baffling industrial urban society. Let us examine these changes in some detail, remembering that there is still much to be learned about the 40-odd million American families in this country and that research is just beginning to answer some of our questions.

A major shortcoming of the diagnoses formulated by writers in the mass media is the fact that they have been based on a limited number of observations. The psychiatrists drew primarily from the biased sample of cases they observed in clinical practice. Judges are prone to write from the distorted view of marriages sick enough for couples to seek adjudication of their troubles through divorce. Other writers relied heavily on the accumulated personal contacts of a lifetime of shrewd observations, often involving no more than a hundred families all told. I hope to improve on this by turning to the several research studies and surveys by social scientists in recent years covering several thousand families, and the findings of the censuses and sample surveys of the Bureau of the Census which cover the country as a whole.

In quick review I hope to answer three major questions: 1) What long-term and what short-term changes are occur-

ring in marriage and family patterns in America? 2) Is the
family any less important to its members and to American
society today than formerly? and 3) What are some implications for conference discussion and for social action of these
changes in family patterns?

Changes in Marriage and Family Patterns

A number of changes in the family tend to be tied to the
highly interrelated phenomena of industrialization, urbanization, secularization, and democratization. These we term
long-run trends since they have been more or less continuous
and cumulative in their impact on family patterns since well
before the Civil War. Another set of changes should be desig-
nated as short term because they tend to be relatively temporary fluctuations around a long-term trend line. They may
occur as a consequence of changes in the age and sex com-
position of the population, or may flow from the vacillations
of the country's economy and polity best seen in the cycles
of depression and prosperity, of inflation and deflation, and
hot wars and cold wars.

As a backdrop for discussing long-term trends let us identify the typical family pattern of a century ago when we were
largely a rural frontier society. There were, to be sure, several
coexisting minority family patterns which differed in some
respects, the colorful but numerically insignificant plantation
family of the Southern upper class to mention only one. John
Sirjamaki is our source:

The majority family of the nineteenth century tended to be
typically of large size because, although the matter was never

put so crassly, many persons were needed for the ceaseless, back-breaking labor of the farms. In 1790 the median family had 5.4 children, and the birth rate which sustained it, 55 per 1,000 population. This high fertility resulted in such a volume of children that the median age of the population in 1790, the first year in which a federal census was taken, was sixteen years. Relatives of course multiplied in consequence, and the social obligations of kinship were well observed. Kinship was traced bilaterally, that is, on both the male and the female sides of the family, although the former may have been of slightly greater social significance in that it was better supported by the patriarchal practices of the society.

Authority in the majority family was lodged in its male head. European practice and law alike fostered such patriarchy, and American experience appeared to justify it. At any rate, the concentration of power in one person who could organize family members in common enterprise and safeguard their welfare was genuinely necessary in farm life, and this command seemed to rest naturally with the husband and father. His rule was, however, considerably tempered by the fact that women did not always bend easily in obedience to their mates. The rugged frontier existence developed competence and self-reliance in them, and from an early time they had high prestige in frontier society.

The custom of separate domicile by newly wedded couples was adapted to the rural economy of family-sized farmsteads. Such farms were frequently too small to support the related families of two generations, and children upon marriage therefore established themselves apart from parents, often on land or with funds or tools partly provided by them.

Another majority family pattern was the comparative freedom young people exercised in their choice of marriage partners. For a while this was hindered by the requirement that a bride bring a dowry in money, goods, or estate to her husband in marriage. But this custom did not long persist because women, often in short supply, were gladly taken in wedlock without the added lure of a dowry, and many families had little enough property to bestow anyway. Moreover, because the bringing of a dowry was based upon arranged marriages and necessitated haggling over property settlements, it came to seem excessively gauche and unsentimental.

Of the quality of family living in the nineteenth century it is difficult to generalize, since Americans were of many conditions and domestic felicity is never constant or universal. More was then required than now of the family as an institution in the struggle for existence; hence, successful marriages were judged by their permanence, or fertility, or affluence, and less by the private happiness of the mates. Parent-child relationships were amiable, but often, because mothers were kept busy with household chores, older children were required to take charge of the younger ones. . . . But the hardships of frontier existence often reached into family living, constraining it and removing its joy. The struggle to survive was so relentless that family members had to labor ceaselessly. Houses were often meanly built and small, and the standard of living within them low. Loneliness was frequently the fate of many families, especially those on farm and frontier. Many mothers, worn out by excessive childbearing, died in early middle age, average life expectancy was below forty years in the first half of the nineteenth century. Amelioration of many of these hardships eventually arrived with the industrial development of the country, but for some families it was slow in coming and for others it did not come at all.[1]

LONG-TERM TRENDS. One can recognize in this majority family pattern of the nineteenth century many characteristics which have survived into the twentieth century: freedom of mate selection, separate domicile for newlyweds (although one couple in five begin marriage even today in the home of one of the parental families), parental subsidy of marriage (although the support today may need to be more subtle

---

[1] John Sirjamaki, *The American Family in the 20th Century* (Cambridge: Harvard University Press, 1953).

and less openly admitted). In other respects there have been tremendous changes as America has industrialized and urbanized, changes which we identify as long-term trends: changed ways of making a living, decreased self-sufficiency of families, smaller households, increased mobility of families, changed authority patterns, and changed age and sex roles within the family, to mention only a few. Activities once centered in the home, such as production of food and clothing, family recreation, vocational apprenticing, and religious instruction, have been shifted to canneries, factories, recreation centers, vocational schools, and Sunday Schools.

From 1890 to 1960 the proportion of American families subsisting from farming changed from almost half to less than one-tenth. With this changed mode of making a living, the authoritarian, economically integrated, self-sufficient form of family which for centuries had been functionally adapted to rural living has become obsolete. As the family ceased to be a producer of goods and services, the need for an authoritarian foreman in the family disappeared. But as the family ceased to make its own living, and the father left the home to earn money to buy the goods the family once produced, the self-sufficiency of the family also disappeared. The rugged familism which extended the frontier and gave the tenor of individualism to America has disappeared except as it is found in isolated rural and mountain areas.

The family became dependent upon the availability of jobs, on continued prosperity, and on the productivity of the wage earner. Where the father's productivity was not great enough, mothers left the home to supplement the father's pay check. Children, once viewed as potential added hands who soon could earn their keep, have become in the industrial age mouths to feed, bodies to clothe, and minds to educate. Today children are financial liabilities from birth through their schooling. Conservative estimates place the cost of rearing a child to age eighteen at $20,000, and there is still his college education ahead of him.

In order to get ahead in the world young families have become mobile, migrating for added education, better jobs, and in response to the demands of military service. Compared with other countries of the world we are a people on wheels— 1 family in 5 moves annually and 1 in 3 of these crosses county lines every year.

In the course of these long-term shifts in the economy and the larger society the family has given up many services it once provided its members: schooling, religious instruction, recreation, medical care, and job placement. Many see in these changes evidences of family decay and disorganization, but I find abundant proof that there is no repudiation of the basic business of families; namely, reproduction, housing, feeding, socializing, and guiding children from infancy to adulthood. Indeed, the family is now more of a specialized agency concentrating on personality development of its members, providing warmth, love, and sanctuary from the anonymity of urban existence, services no other agency in society is prepared to offer.

SHORT-RUN CHANGES. Let us turn now for a moment to the examination of some short-run changes which have occurred in recent years. Family behavior has become increasingly subject to short-run fluctuations integrally related to the economic and political shifts in our highly interdependent type of society. Individuals are increasingly making their marital and reproductive decisions deliberately, taking into account their personal outlook of the moment. The result is often that millions make the same kind of decision at the same time. If conditions are bad as they were during the depression of the '30s, for example, people postpone marriage or if married put off childbearing. At that time hundreds of thousands of young women, after waiting for several years to marry, had to face the specter of spinsterhood because the men, when they did marry, turned to a younger age group for their brides. Later when conditions improved, young people who might have waited decided to marry, or if married decided to have children, and the marriage rates and birth rates responded violently.

The propensity to marry has been so affected by the prosperity of the past decade and a half that a greater increase in the proportion of the population married has occurred than in the previous half century. Among men twenty to twenty-four years of age the proportion married nearly doubled from 1940 to 1955, from 27 percent to 51 percent. Among women of the same ages the percentage married also increased sharply, from 51 percent to 70 percent. The number of marriages in America during the war and postwar years has been increasing very rapidly, only divorce among the vital statistics being more volatile.

Divorce has been subject both to long-term and short-term changes. The long-term trend has been on the increase since the first census covering divorce in 1870, reflecting among other things the emancipation of women through education and industrialization. As a short-term phenomenon the divorce rate follows the marriage rate, which in turn reflects so closely the fluctuations of the business cycle. A cynic once said the basic cause of divorce is marriage! It is true that when marriage rates are low as in a depression so is divorce, and when marriage rates go up so does divorce, for most divorces occur in the early years of marriage. Henry Bowman has used the analogy of a great throng of people on an open drawbridge. As more crowd to get on, others fall off the open end into the water below.

Divorce reached a high of one divorce for every two and one-half marriages in 1946 and has since declined to one in five marriages (the lowest figure since 1941), in line with the more recent decline in the marriage rate. Most vulnerable to divorce during this period have been the childless, the teen-age couples, veterans, the grammar-school educated, and low income groups. Not only are grammar-school educated persons more likely to become divorced (the rate is twice that of persons with a college education), but they end their marriages on the average nine years earlier than college people who do divorce.

A corollary trend which is noteworthy is the high rate of remarriage of the divorced, three-fourths of whom marry again within five years, and 87 percent of whom eventually remarry. Most likely to remarry are divorcees whose first marriage occurred before the age of eighteen. We are in effect operating a type of trial marriage system in this country in which the first marriage breaks in and domesticates the parties, and the second marriage reaps the benefits.[2] The remarriage rate is good evidence that the high rate of divorce in our society constitutes no repudiation of marriage itself. Marriage has never been more popular; about 70 percent of the population between the ages of fourteen to ninety were married in 1958. Eighteen percent were single and most of them will eventually marry. Eight percent were widowed, 3 percent separated, and only 2 percent were in divorced status.

A British social scientist commented on these statistics: "You Americans talk a lot about divorce, but in Europe we worry about the fact that people don't bother to marry. Over 90 percent eventually marry in America, but only 70 percent do in Sweden and Switzerland, and fewer yet in Ireland. The age at first marriage of men in rural Ireland is almost forty, more than ten years later than in America." Americans have indeed been very legal in their channeling of the sex drive in wedlock. They have had low rates of illegal cohabitation, concubinage is unheard of, and common law unions are rare. Yet we have one of the highest rates of change of married partners of any Western civilization. Paul Landis has called our form of marriage serial polygyny! You may wish to reverse it and call it brittle monogamy.

Let us turn to another trend which like divorce looks different when viewed as a long-term than when viewed as a short-run phenomenon—namely, the size of completed families.

[2] A highly readable serious study of second and third marriages of the divorced and widowed is Jessie Bernard's Remarriage (New York: Dryden Press, 1956).

Since frontier days the size of households has been shrinking steadily. In 1700, 7.4 children had been born to the average mother forty-five years of age and over. By 1910 the number had dropped to 4.7, by 1940 to 2.9, and by 1950 to 2.5 children.

A reversal of this long-term trend is in the making as a consequence of the prolongation of the baby boom of the 1940s and '50s. When a boom continues beyond ten years it begins to look like a trend. The increase in the birth rate was a direct result of the rapid increases in marriages of the war and postwar years beginning first with many more first babies, later with more second and third babies, and now fourth babies. Since 1950 the number of first babies has declined sharply just as the marriage rate has, both examples of short-run changes, but the number of second babies has held up, and third and fourth babies continue to increase. Comparing 1940–41 with 1954–55 the birth rate of third and fourth babies is up 70 percent.

The shift in family size, however, is not to large families of seven or more children, which have continued to decline from 15 percent of completed families in 1910 to less than 4 percent of completed families in 1957. Childlessness, at the other extreme, is also in decline, having dropped from 20 percent in 1940 to less than 10 percent in 1957. A recent nation-wide study [3] could uncover no interest in childless or one-child families and found the most favored family size to be between three and four children. In successive polls the

[3] Ronald Freedman, Pascal K. Whelpton, and Arthur A. Campbell, *Family Planning, Sterility, and Population Growth* (New York: McGraw-Hill, 1959).

proportion favoring the four-child family has increased from
20 percent in 1941 to 41 percent in 1955, while the proportion favoring two children has declined from 40 to 19 percent
over the same period. This same study provides evidence
that the higher birth rates of the last fifteen years and the
prevailing favorable climate for medium-size families will
soon affect completed family size in the United States. Asking women not yet forty-five years of age how many more
children they expect to have, the researchers found women
born 1916–20 (who reach the end of childbearing in 1960–64)
have had or expect to have 2.9 children, women born 1921–
25 expect 3.0 children, and women born 1931–37 expect 3.2
children, which is substantially more than the 2.4 children
produced by mothers who had completed their childbearing
by 1950. It is rather exciting to see a long-term trend change
directions.

Closely related to the trend of number of children is the
pattern of spacing children, which has undergone some
changes with the widespread use of birth control. There is
now a tendency to bunch all the children in the early years
of marriage, so that women complete childbearing in their
late twenties and early thirties. The average mother in the
United States in 1950 had her last child at age twenty-six.
Coupled with an earlier age at marriage for husbands, which
has dropped in sixty years from 26.1 to 22.6 and for women
from 22.0 to 20.4, husband and wife have a much longer
period of companionship together than their parents enjoyed.
With her children in school by the time she is in her early
thirties, the wife is freer to re-enter the labor force—40 per-

cent of wives aged thirty to forty with children in school are gainfully employed. Indeed, there has been a 77 percent increase in married women ages thirty-five to forty-four in the labor force in the last decade.

Needless to say, this shortening of the period in which the husband must be the sole breadwinner makes marriage less of a financial commitment for men and brings to the relation a more companionate quality. The traditional sentiment that a new husband must support his wife as her father did has now been attenuated in nearly all strata of our society by the growing desire of wives to share in their husbands' financial struggles.

CHANGES IN SEX ROLES. As a consequence of these many changes—younger age at marriage, changes in child spacing, as well as changed ways of making a living and the changed emphasis on services performed in the family—the relationships between husband and wife and between children and parents have changed sharply with respect to the locus of power and in the division of duties and responsibilities in the family. Wives and children are becoming economic partners with the husband-father in spending as well as in earning the family income. The family is becoming democratized in the process.

Participation by wives in family decision making extends beyond financial matters and is concurrently being strengthened by their higher education, wider contact outside the home, exercise of responsibility in civic associations, activities in professional organizations, and by explicit encouragement by experts. Male pretensions to superior authority are widely ridiculed in contemporary comedy, cartoons, children's literature, and other forms of popular art. Moreover, when family decision making is viewed as a symbol of power the superiority of shared power in creating and maintaining warmth and affection becomes evident. It is easier to love a reasonable, companionable man, and harder to love an authoritarian husband and father today.

Equally striking in the blurring of sex lines are the changes in the division of tasks and responsibilities in the home. Here the middle classes lead the way, according to a recent study covering hundreds of Omaha families at various educational and occupational status levels. The investigator asked who was primarily responsible for the performance of each of a hundred homely tasks that must be performed to keep a family going. His findings may be stated briefly:

1. The middle classes have gone farthest in bringing the husband into taking responsibility for family tasks, and also designate more tasks as the *joint responsibility* of husband and wife.

2. The lower classes placed more of the burdens on the mother and the children, while the upper classes were the only group to turn to outside help for any substantial proportion of family jobs.

3. For all classes, to be sure, the majority pattern is for the wife to assume responsibility for the greatest number of tasks (40–50 percent). Second most popular pattern is that of *joint responsibility* (25–28 percent); third in line is the hus-

band assuming chief responsibility for 20–23 percent of tasks, followed by children with 6–10 percent, and outside help 1–14 percent of tasks.

4. Joint responsibility was the majority pattern for certain types of tasks involving especially control and decision making, such as disciplining children, training in manners, supervising school work, deciding when to buy a new car, planning the budget, and so on.

There remain today only two or three tasks securely monopolized by one sex: childbearing and sewing by the wife, and the most arduous physical maintenance chores by the husband. Painting, repairing, fueling, and car washing are increasingly taken on by the wife, sometimes alone, often with the husband. Her dress on these occasions will be male work clothes and her language will also often be appropriate to the task!

The same crossing of ancient boundaries by the husband is also fast becoming commonplace—diaper changing, dishwashing, cooking, house cleaning, laundering, and shopping are duties shared with the wife, especially if she is gainfully employed—and he has learned to wear an apron, a butcher's apron, to be sure, but an apron! Such sharing of tasks fluctuates, rotates, and changes unevenly, frequently provoking conflict, but the net effect is greater companionship between husband and wife and more freedom for later leisure time pursuits together. Some women and men resent this as a usurpation of their prerogatives, indeed some feel bereaved of function, but most welcome it.

Still another source of marital integration is the trend in

America to undertake leisure time pursuits together. Except in family enterprises like farming, or small family retail enterprises, very few couples have been able to coordinate their work lives at the same vocation, but the decline of segregated amusements "for men only" and "for women only" in favor of recreation for couples more than offsets this handicap. It has become impolite to invite husbands only or wives only to most social functions; today as a consequence agreement upon friends and outside interests now appears as important in predicting marital adjustment as approval by the parental families once did. It appears probable that the urban husband spends more hours per week in the company of his wife than in any decade since factories removed manufacturing of goods from the home. Recreation and social activities now integrate the sexes.

But companionship in marriage is more than sharing common tasks in the home and participating in common leisure time activities. Nelson Foote has advanced the concept of "matching careers" to describe the phenomenon of mutual stimulation to development which occurs in a highly companionable marriage.

To expect a marriage to last indefinitely under modern conditions is to expect a lot. The conception of marriage as continually requiring the incitement of new episodes of shared activity will have more consequences than can be foreseen, but a few implications can perhaps be inferred. Happiness as a criterion of success, for instance, is inherently unstable over time. And even at a given time, the prospect of future achievement of aims may have more effect on the judgment of a marriage by its partners than their current state of gratification. Certainly marriage counselors report many cases of mates who

disclose no specific cause of dissatisfaction yet complain that
they have lost interest in their marriages. Successful marriage
may thus come to be defined, both by married people and by
students of marriage, in terms of its potential for continued
development, rather than in terms of momentary assessments of
adjustment. . . .

In particular the notion of matching careers need not imply
that husband and wife pursue identical professional careers outside the home. . . . Though their careers be differentiated both
in and out of the home, the point that seems decisive in understanding the quality of their marriages appears to remain in the
degree of matching in their phases of distinct but comparable
development. A simple test may be this, how much do they have
to communicate when they are together? [4]

How is this self-conscious appetite for a marriage that will
lead to further development of the partners distributed
within the occupational classes? Our information on this
question is inadequate, but it would appear that it is primarily
in the professional classes that companionship and mutual
development is sought. In rural and working classes the relative prominence of functional economic interdependence as
the basis for family stability seems much greater than in the
more leisured white-collar, business, and professional levels.
Moreover, the trend is for more and more of the working
force to move from agriculture and manufacturing into the
services. If in turn they shift in their interests in marriage to
the focus of the professional classes the implications for
family stability are provocative, for repeated studies show

[4] Nelson N. Foote, "Matching of Husband and Wife in Phases of
Development," in *Transactions of the Third World Congress of Sociology* (London: International Sociological Association, 1956), IV, 29.

that the professional classes are the least vulnerable to divorce of all occupational strata.[5]

The standard view that industrialization and urbanization are inexorably destructive of family stability and solidarity is thus contradicted by the fact that the professional group, which has a low divorce rate, is also the fullest beneficiary of such aspects of industrialism and urbanism as the reliance on science, spatial and social mobility, and emphasis on the welfare and freedom of the individual. The professional group is most liberal in its views about divorce, and is most egalitarian in its views on the propriety of employment of married women and in espousing the notion of equal authority for husband and wife within the family. It appears to be the most cosmopolitan in the range of its choice of marriage mates; most heterogamous in crossing ethnic, class, and religious lines; least affected by propinquity and closest in ages at marriage. It would seem that voluntary commitments emphasized by the professional groups may be stronger bonds for marriage than the economic and legal sanctions which held together traditional families. To adapt an old saying, what is poison to the rural, traditional family may be meat to the urban, professional family.[6]

PROFESSIONALIZATION OF FAMILY ROLES. What do these trends I have cited add up to? Increasing specialization by the family in services performed for its members, increased

[5] W. J. Goode, *After Divorce* (Glencoe, Ill.: The Free Press, 1956), see especially Chapters IV and V, which summarize these studies, pp. 43–67.
[6] Foote, in *Transactions of Third World Congress of Sociology*, IV, 30.

emphasis on quality of performance, shift in focus from production of goods to interest in personality development of children, and high affirmation of companionship in marriage and parent-child relations. Possibly Nelson Foote's term, "The Professionalization of Marital and Family Roles," describes best what is taking place in America today.

Marriage is increasingly viewed as a kind of joint career for which preparation can provide the skills and insights to achieve success. Miller and Swanson have been tempted to call the emerging family the "colleague" family. "As specialists at work may find in each other skills they lack, but skills they equally need, and as they may defer to one another's judgment on the grounds of different competence without feeling that they have personally lost in prestige, so husband and wife may now relate in this way." [7] They see this trend toward specialization leading to the professionalization of the wife's functions. She can no longer learn them satisfactorily from her mother's tutelage and example; they must be rationalized. Intuitive processes give way to formal rules and special technical knowledge. Moreover, the skills employed are subject to improvement as they are submitted to critical appraisal and functional selection. In career terms, the women's magazines provide a kind of in-service training, supplemented with the postgraduate work of the mother study clubs, the meetings with the specialists at the nursery school, the cooking classes, and the growing number of handbooks for preparing unfamiliar or exotic foods.[8] The rise of

[7] Daniel R. Miller and Guy E. Swanson, *The Changing American Parent* (New York: Wiley, 1958), pp. 200–1.

[8] Miller and Swanson, *Changing American Parent*, p. 201.

college and high-school courses in preparation for marriage and parenthood attended by men as well as women and the development of counseling services further affirm this desire on the part of young people to get professional training for their marital and parental roles.

Planning for parenthood today actually goes beyond planning for the control of conception, although a recent nation-wide study reveals that children born today are more likely than ever to be wanted, planned children. They are more likely to be seen as a fulfillment rather than a frustration of marriage goals today than in the depression and post-depression period. Planning for parenthood today includes programs of education for parenthood to facilitate the understanding of children in general and one's own children in particular and thereby to help parents contribute to the maximum development of their personalities. This is a trend of vast significance for personality development and mental health.

Not only are parents professionalizing their marital and parental roles, they are undertaking once again training of the child for the job world, not by providing technical skills but by helping him in human relations. The child must learn the nuances of interpersonal relations to function in the large and complex organizations of industry, business, and government. The child must study his own relations to others and gain better control over himself and his associates. Parents in the professions today do have relevant, hard-bought skills to make the critical judgments of social situations that their children will need. Miller and Swanson expect, moreover, a reappearance of the parent as the counselor and aid of his children after they have become adults and parents in their own right, thus enabling children to serve as a means of self-continuity and companionship as well as fulfillment.[9] In sum, parents have learned that in the contemporary world, a parent is far better advised to endow his child with competence in interpersonal relations than to leave him with "a competence" in the old sense of the word.

How Important Is the Family Today?

With this background in the vast changes that have occurred in the American family, how should we answer my second question, Is the family any less important to its members and to American society than formerly?

It must be granted that the present-day family is not the giant in numbers and functions that it was a century ago. We no longer count as members of our families our kin out to third cousins on either side, and often forget both sets of grandparents and any great-grandparents when we reckon our family size. The modern family, shorn of kinship attachments and bearing two to four children, is smaller and less of an all-purpose organization—but is it therefore less important?

It would be a mistake to assume that because many families are free floating and geographically rootless, most urban families are separated from significant supportive relationships. Recent studies in London, Detroit, Cleveland, and Minneapolis attest to the perseverance of reciprocal relation-

[9] Miller and Swanson, *Changing American Parent*, p. 204.

ships of gift giving, visiting, mutual aid, and advice seeking between grandparents and their married children, and between nuclear families and their kinfolk. In charting the social network of families they still tend to list relatives above friends and neighbors as the first place to turn when crisis strikes.

Yet there have also been social losses in the streamlining and specializing of the modern family. The modern nuclear family focuses primarily on the maintenance of the marriage and the provision of services to the immediate offspring of the marriage. In specializing, the family has not only given up *services* once provided by the traditional family but it has given up *people* who once could find a meaningful place there: maiden aunts, bachelor uncles, widowed and orphaned kin, and grandparents. As a consequence, many more individuals today live outside organized family groups in semi-isolation from the love and support families might give them.

American families are on the whole probably happier than they were in earlier times, yet so much is asked of marriage and the family today that many otherwise sound families experience relative deprivation. The standards of success today go beyond providing and getting ahead economically, beyond the maintenance of minimum goals of health and education for children, to include happiness and self-realization. Few families appear to measure up, yet every man regards a happy marriage as his right. The defects of the modern family develop primarily from the disabilities of the specific persons who marry and rear children. If greater stability of the family is ever to be assured, increasing the competence of young people in interpersonal relations and selecting people for marriage who are ready for parental responsibilities must be undertaken much more systematically.

Granting that marriages today are intrinsically less enduring, evidence can be brought to show that they are greatly improved in quality of performance and are more stimulating climates in which to rear children. In addition, the modern family has the virtue of fitting well the demands of our democratic and urban industrial society, something that would have been impossible to the larger, rooted, and authoritarian family of the past century.

Since the modern family is smaller, it is more mobile, moving where opportunities are to be found. The medium-sized family fits the occupational structure better, relying as it does on achievement on the job over kinship preference for getting ahead in the job world. Small nuclear families of husband, wife, and children, as contrasted with great extended families of the past, appear to be ideally adapted to the different degrees of social movement required by our open competitive type of class society—permitting movement both horizontally in geographic space and vertically in climbing the occupational ladder.

Extended families of the past, in sharp contrast, tended to standardize a single class status among all family members and impose barriers of vested family interests to thwart the principle of equal opportunities of all persons to strive for social mobility. To be sure, parents in nuclear families also confer their own class position initially upon their children, but this transfer of status is never sure or permanent, and eventually must be earned in occupational achievement. Great extended families have in the past constituted a threat to the integrity of public service, undermining democratic processes and the principles of career civil service by nepotistic manipulation of government in behalf of family members. They would seem to be much less well adapted to the economic and political structure of our contemporary society than present-day nuclear type families which are too small to participate in coalitions or to build pyramids of power within business or government.

Is the family any less important to American society than formerly? By virtue of its specialization and its close adaptation to the economic and political structure, the family fits contemporary American society remarkably well. Moreover, the modern family is fully as needed today as formerly since it has no serious competitors among the other agencies in our society for the performance of the personality-building functions in which it is currently specializing. We depend almost exclusively on the family today for the performance of the vital functions of reproduction, infant care, and socialization, without which our society would disintegrate.

Implications for Social Action

What are some implications for discussion and social action of the changes in family patterns we have identified? Two specific changes in family patterns require our attention.

HIGH MOBILITY AND NEIGHBORHOOD DEVELOPMENT. Although nonmobile families continue to maintain a nest of

kin and neighbors within which they can function in reciprocal assistance and support, what of the mobile families who
have separated themselves by geographic movement from
kin and home town neighbors? To whom do they turn for
counsel and help when they want to spill their troubles?
How do they become integrated into a new neighborhood or
community? The high mobility of young families results in
feelings of "aloneness" and "lockedupness" as they move
into new communities or join the stream moving out of the
central city into the suburbs.

The challenge is to develop institutions less commercial
than the "welcome wagon" and more neighborhood oriented.
We need community organization and neighborhood development activities in this direction such as Milwaukee supported for a time. We need to institutionalize the status of
"newcomers" and utilize it to provide orientation and wel-
coming activities into neighborhood and community.

DIVORCE ADJUSTMENT AND SOCIAL AMBIGUITIES. The high
rate of divorce and remarriage suggests the need for attention
to inventing ways of easing postdivorce adjustment and facili-
tating successful remarriages. We are better prepared to deal
with bereavement of widows and widowers than we are with
the adjustments of the divorced. For example, there are no
ethical imperatives for relatives or friends that would make
them feel constrained to furnish material or emotional support during or after the divorce to the divorced. There is no
clear definition of responsibility for readmitting divorce participants back into their former statuses as members of the
parental family. Pathways to forming new male or female

friendships and remarriage are poorly charted, and there is a distinct ambiguity concerning the proper behavior of the spouses after the divorce. Do they remain forever distant and alienated, or do they re-establish friendships for the children's sake? These ambiguities beg clarification.

NEED FOR NATIONAL AND LOCAL POLICIES FOR FAMILY WELL-BEING. There is still another dimension in which we can move in conference discussion, the dimension of recommending national and local policies for family well-being. The United States is one of the few civilized countries of the world which has not yet formulated an explicit family policy on which a coherent program for families could be built. The federal government, having ceded the issues of family life to the states, has taken little initiative in promoting programs of family betterment. Indeed, the constitution writers avoided the problem by failing to acknowledge the family as a legal entity. Since the issues of family life have few interstate ramifications they have appeared beyond the power of the federal arm of government. Consequent to the denial to the federal government of powers related to the family, we have fifty states with conflicting laws controlling marriage, divorce, responsibility of parents to children, and so on.

It took years of depression to bring the recognition to legislators that family self-sufficiency was no longer feasible in an industrial economy, and that no family can be held entirely responsible for its own destiny. The various extensions of the Social Security Act are important steps toward expanding the role of government in shoring up family resources, but this is only the beginning of a national policy for family life. It seems not incorrect to suggest that the principles of laissez faire have been applied to the relation of government and families with considerably more success than is true in the case of government and business. No pressure group has yet made of government a positive instrument for the benefit of family life. A family policy for America would include not only general goals but specific means appropriate for their realization.

FIVE RECOMMENDATIONS FOR ACTION. In conclusion, may I share with you selected recommendations for action which Dr. Emily H. Mudd, director of the Marriage Council of Philadelphia, and I obtained in an idea-getting survey of sixteen selected practitioners from the major disciplines influencing family life in the United States three years ago. They are embodied in a memorandum prepared for the Commissioner of the Social Security Administration, at his initiative and with his active collaboration.

1. The recommendations begin with a proposal for education for family life at every stage of human development, timed at critical points of maximum readiness when members are most teachable.

   a) It is felt that education has the virtue of intervening before trouble strikes, that it is preventive and helps families help themselves. Moreover, education can be carried out in a variety of settings by social workers, marriage counselors, and writers, as well as teachers.

2. A second recommendation on which there was high consensus among members of our interview panel involved

ways of intervening to improve family life through the courts and legal agencies of government.

   a) Uniform marriage and divorce laws were urged which would prevent hasty marriages and impulsive divorces.

   b) Enabling legislation empowering domestic relations courts to provide counseling services was also recommended.

3. Guidance and remedial measures were recommended, although there was a noticeable reluctance to make them the primary emphasis in future program planning.

   a) Marriage counseling and mental health clinics were recommended for every community, possibly in the neighborhood high school where everyone would feel free to come.

4. A fourth cluster of recommendations appears novel indeed and refers to the need to build the morale of family members engaged in the significant task of rearing the nation's children.

   a) Family morale might be strengthened with a government department which protects family interests as the interests of labor, commerce, and agriculture are already protected—particularly against the stresses which emanate from government policies affecting inflation, unemployment, selective service, and war.

   b) A White House Conference on Family Life to lay the groundwork for a national policy for families would surely have the effect of improving family morale in the United States.

5. A final suggestion involves programs of training and re-fresher work for the personnel of the family-serving agencies of the country. Such programs would consider ways of relating the agencies to families so as to facili-tate family development rather than to defeat them. If families are to be strengthened rather than weakened as a consequence of contact with helping agencies, what principles might guide workers?

a) Workers will do best who permit high participation by families in setting the goals and determining the out-come of service by involvement of all family members on a group basis.

b) Workers and family members are optimally engaged if they are dedicated to bringing about *full family development* rather than the restoration of any pre-conceived status quo.

c) To reach this high goal, workers should actively seek to make available their professional insights and secrets to family members in the interest of leaving parents and children better able to cope with the task of be-coming an adequate and effective family.

These proposals may seem ambitious to some but are merely suggestive of the kind of help which agencies can offer for improving the performance of American families. I see the family, with these aids, surviving even the amazing tech-nological developments now being forecast for the atomic age, and surviving the impact of urbanization, of social mobility, of wars and economic depressions, with a minimum of scars and a maximum of vitality. I see great possibilities in the family of tomorrow as an improved medium-sized family organization, geared to assure maximum self-expression of family members while maintaining integrity and inner loyalty to the whole. My optimism is predicated on the universality of the family phenomenon, on its survival powers in the past, on its present adaptability, and on the anticipated shape of things to come.

THE CHANGING NEGRO FAMILY

by HYLAN LEWIS

IN *An American Dilemma* (1944), Gunnar Myrdal began the section, "The Negro Family," in this way: "The recent book by E. Franklin Frazier, *The Negro Family in the United States* (1939), is such an excellent description and analysis . . . that it is practically necessary only to relate its conclusions to our context and to refer the reader to it for details." Twenty-one years after Frazier's classic treatment, Myrdal's acknowledgement and recommendation are still highly appropriate, especially if one wishes to understand the forces that have shaped the Negro family, and its various expressions, in American life and its responsiveness to economic and social changes.

There have been significant changes in the pace and scope of change since this study was made. These make it the more regrettable that the expected revision of Frazier's basic work is not yet available.

This chapter is not an effort to bring earlier studies of the Negro family up to date, but rather, an effort to examine

Hylan Lewis is Program Director, Child Rearing Study, Health and Welfare Council of the National Capital Area.

and interpret family structure, functions, roles, and values among Negroes, mainly in the context of changes that have occurred, matured, or become salient in American society during the last ten years. There is a concern for what these mean or might mean for the larger community, as well as for the Negro family.

A significant part of the recent expansion of the economy, and of related changes in economic organization and control, and in the social and political climate were stimulated and made more urgent by commitments and pressures inherent in the United States' new international role as leader and partner of non-Communist nations. Negro individuals, families, and organizations—and segments of the total population interested in or committed to improvement—now have increased leverage for their efforts, additional alternatives, and increased flexibility. And they are likely to function now, and to plan for the future, with sharply revised estimates of what is possible and what is probable.

Desegregation

The net effects of recently stepped-up rates of change in processes which for a long while have been changing the United States, and the Negro family in particular—specifically the trend towards desegregation—have been beneficial for the country as well as for the Negro segment of its population. However, the effects of these changes are unevenly spread, and involve considerable lag, disorganization, waste, and anxiety. These reflect "the disorganization of transition" as well as the heavy heritage of inequality.

In estimating any improvement in well-being or participation in the American economy, the base from which Negro gains must be measured is smaller than for the white population. The Negro group as a whole is handicapped by a smaller base of social capital and experience, a higher incidence of problems and unused potential, and "sticky" but unevenly spread discrimination. In a sobering estimate, Ginzberg points out: "Within the short span of fifteen years, the economic opportunities of the Negro have vastly increased. Yet, complacency is unwarranted, for even in the cities of the North and West the Negro is far from having equality of opportunity. . . . No matter how rapid the migration from Southern farms continues to be, the birth rate there is so high that large numbers of Negroes will undoubtedly continue to till the soil for several generations." The task in the urban South is to increase the kinds and quality of the jobs open to Negroes: "Their position in Southern industry today is not too different from what it was in many sectors of the North twenty and thirty years ago. . . . At present most jobs available to them in Southern industry lead nowhere." Outside of the South, "large numbers of employers still refuse to hire Negroes. This is particularly true in the major fields of female employment, many of which have only recently been opened to Negro girls and women. Furthermore, even in the North, the majority of Negroes are still concentrated in jobs which are not likely to lead to advancement. These are serious problems, but progress toward solving them is already substantial." [1]

[1] Eli Ginzberg, *The Negro Potential* (New York: Columbia University Press, 1956), pp. 40–41.

Confronted with a current picture and an outlook that combine shadows and light, it is neither surprising nor inconsistent that individual Negro families should exhibit both identification with and detachment from the lumped characteristics and the perceived chances of the Negro as a category—the modal picture. Recent changes, particularly those accompanying urbanization and desegregation, have made it more practicable, and possibly more urgent, for individual Negro families to try to detach themselves in aspirations and conduct from the conventional image of the modal Negro. This probably reflects not so much a denial of the Negro or "Negroness" as such, as it does a denial or repudiation of a single-mode picture or some of its implications for them.

The problem of identity and, therefore, the function of family in relation to it comes now to be less that of training children and adults to live as Negroes in a restricted, but slowly changing, world with a traditional set of rules; and more that of preparation for a world in which the public rules and practices are changing rapidly, and inevitably— albeit unevenly and reluctantly. It is, and promises to be even more, a world in which being a Negro does not as frequently mean automatic discrimination and arbitrary exclusion.

It is also a world in which the chances are better of correcting images of oneself, one's group, and of other groups and other individuals. Shortly after Central High School in Little Rock was integrated in 1958, Kenneth Clark asked one of the nine Negro students involved what was the most important lesson she had learned as a result of her experience.

Clark reports her answering in a rather deliberate manner: "When I used to go to Horace Mann School I thought that white people were different. When I saw the colored kids at Horace Mann acting silly or doing something that I didn't think they should do, I guessed they used to do this because they were colored. Now that I am at Central High School I see the white children do silly things, too. Just like there are some dumb colored children there are some dumb whites. There are some average colored and there are some average whites, and there are some smart whites and some smart colored. I guess what I have learned is that they are not so different and we aren't so different."

Something of one type and level of parental involvement is suggested in this added observation: "When her father suggested that maybe she was working a little harder on her school work than she worked at Horace Mann, she refused to accept this and insisted that she worked as hard as she could at Horace Mann and she is working as hard as she can at Central High School. She stated this with firm matter-of-fact conviction and her father had to accept her interpretation in spite of the fact that it did not agree with his."

It is probably easier for the Negro family and person to live with the fact of being Negro, but there is more anxiety about being or becoming the "right" Negro—and citizen.

The problems of socialization and adjustment in this more fluid society may temporarily be more difficult and productive of anxieties in Negro families on all levels. This is because of the very fact that the social scene will continue to exhibit, and sometimes chaotically, elements of the old and new. There is acute need for some families—and potential need for all—to reconcile the conflict between the values of protection and security; and dignity, advance, and innovation. Greater freedom of choice and movement and the recognition of the potentiality of a better life improve morale. They also make persons more acutely sensitive about the persistent modal image and its factual basis. And they increase dissatisfactions over the fact that changes are not occurring in some areas. It seems reasonable to believe that new developments and trends related to desegregation and enlarged opportunities (and challenges) force the Negro family to take a more direct and positive role in helping the child and young adult define and interpret that world and their chances in it.

There is reason to believe that heretofore the Negro family itself, characteristically, has not directly or systematically provided the child with its education in race. The need to do this directly now is greater—the occasions are more numerous and public; and importantly, it can be done with less ambivalence and shame. How the Negro family meets this challenge and opportunity is the crucial question.

One of the significant aspects of recent developments has been the key role of government in reaffirming the rights of Negroes and in moving to improve opportunities both as a matter of law and morals and national and community self-interest. Connected with these are the underscoring of the Negro's need and disposition to look toward, and use, the national government, and local and state governments where his vote is a factor, for assistance in erasing disabilities in education, housing, employment, public facilities, and courts of law.

The Negro family necessarily reflects and is affected more frequently by a pragmatic linkage of key wants and expectations to government. Affected in varying degree are its sharing of public education in the South and North; its chances and hopes for better housing; and its access to some jobs and industries. And of course it is touched disproportionately by the law and social agencies because of higher dependancy, crime, delinquency, and illegitimacy rates—and just the physical fact of being slum dwellers.

Since this involvement is tactical, rather than ideological, it would be interesting to investigate the social-psychological implications of this for the future of Negro family functions and values.

New Urban Frontiers

The main frontier on which the Negro family will shape, and have shaped, its forms and functions and make its contributions to American life is the city. And it is in the city that we can see written now the effects of the rapid influx of new migrants, increased occupational mobility, educational improvement, and desegregation of public services and facilities on all Negro families.

Urbanization means, particularly for the new migrants from rural areas, the beginnings of a kind of delayed acculturation, introduction of more Negro wage earners into the non-agricultural labor force, better educational opportunities, increased political participation and power, and more direct sharing in public welfare and protective services. It also means immediate acute problems for both old and new Negro families, and for the white population. However, the economic, political, and social imperatives of urban life are such that the Negro family in the city gets an automatic increment in the struggle for realization and recognition merely by the fact of being there.

The recent rapid urbanization has affected Negro families unevenly and in a variety of ways. One reason is that all of the movement is not that of poorly educated, unsophisticated rural persons and families. It is likely, despite their generally poor background, that recent migrants are on the whole better equipped than their predecessors of a generation or more ago. Yet, they are relatively at a greater disadvantage because of changes in the quality of the demand for workers in industry, service, and commerce. On the other hand, particularly in the urban communities of the North and West, their public rights and interests are better protected—if for no other reason than the political strength of Negroes already settled in those communities.

Today, 2 out of every 3 Negroes live in urban areas; and more than one-third of all Negroes now live in urban areas outside of the South. If present trends continue, it is estimated that by the end of the next fifteen years one-fourth to one-third of the population of a number of the larger cities, and as much as one-fifth of the population of some of the larger metropolitan areas will be Negro. An extreme example, and special case in many ways, is Washington, D.C., where Negroes now represent about 45 percent of the population.

About 9 out of every 10 Negroes in the nation's capital live in the central city. Washington is likely to be a predominantly Negro community in 1970. It is important to note that among Southern cities there is a tendency for the proportion of Negroes to decline.

The gross statistics reveal that Negro families in urban areas significantly exceed the total population with respect to rates of residence in older parts of the central city, female heads of families, working wives, sub-families, doubling-up in households, separations, widowhood, illegitimacy, and participation in the Aid to Dependent Children program.

In standard metropolitan areas, approximately 4 out of 5 Negroes live in the central cities in contrast to about 3 out of 5 of the white population. Concentrated in the central parts of metropolitan areas, the Negro family has less housing available. And much of the new housing available is that vacated by whites moving to suburban areas and new developments, from which Negroes are excluded by policy or high costs.

The Negro population increased slightly more than one-sixth between 1940 and 1950, but there was an increase of only one-seventh in the number of their dwelling units. On the other hand, the white population increased about one-seventh and there was an increase of nearly one-fourth in the number of dwelling units.

Between 1940 and 1954, the doubling rate among non-white couples was close to twice that for white couples.[2] The

[2] Many of the family statistics cited here and following are taken or adapted from Paul C. Glick, *American Families* (New York: Wiley, 1957).

significantly higher doubling rate in Negro households is not only a function of lower income, although it is an important factor. It reflects also the smaller supply of housing for all Negroes and the significant role of kinship, particularly among low-income families. As Frazier points out, this does not mean that the urban Negro family has retained the character of an extended family. This is a pragmatic urban cultural form. The rate of doubling for Negroes in 1954 was about the same as the rate for whites in 1940.

Despite the fact that fertility rates are higher for Negro couples than white couples, proportionately fewer Negro sons and daughters under eighteen years old still live with their parents. Larger proportions of Negro youths in their teens live apart from relatives or live in families of relatives other than their parents. This is also true of younger Negro children but to a lesser extent. In urban areas both in and out of the South, the proportion of middle-age Negro families with young sons and daughters in their homes is significantly lower than that for white families. For farm areas, the reverse is true.

The likelihood that a Negro family is a "project dweller" in a public housing unit is much greater than the likelihood that a white family is—and the Negro ratio appears to be increasing. In 1954, Negro families occupied more than a third (37.7 percent) of all such units available; in 1957, the proportion exceeded two-fifths (43.7 percent.) This represents an upgrading of housing for some Negro families. An increasing proportion of low-income urban Negro families are either aspirants to or graduates of public housing projects.

There are many relative gains for Negro families that live in public housing projects, but complaints and invidiousness with respect to these units and their residents are increasing within the Negro community, as well as the larger community.

Public housing continues to be both the first and last best hope of low-income, marginal families, and those involved with social and welfare agencies. The fact that such housing is under attack for a variety of reasons threatens, and increases the invidiousness with respect to, an important setting for a large slice of Negro family life. The gap between the housing project dweller and the rest of the Negro community is likely to widen as general upgrading of living and status standards occurs.

More than 25,000 Negro families are "living under conditions of open-occupancy," according to Public Housing officials. Housing experts point out, however, that experience has shown that where racial barriers in public housing have been broken by public policy or law, there is a tendency for the units to become all-minority.

Negro families are disproportionately involved in the displacement and relocation problems related to slum clearance, urban redevelopment, and urban renewal programs. Overall approximately 2 out of every 3 persons displaced are Negroes. In seventeen communities in the Southeastern Region, for example, 95 percent of the families displaced were Negro; and less than 2 out of 3 of these families were relocated in "decent, safe, and sanitary" houses. One of every 5 families went into substandard housing.

Improved job opportunities and increased incomes since

the 1940s have contributed to the marked increase in home ownership among Negroes and significant upgrading in housing among the middle and upper-income families in urban areas, as a result of both individual efforts and new, privately sponsored but government-insured housing projects for Negroes. Despite this improvement, with the increased population and concentration in the central city, the housing market for the Negro family continues severely restricted. The chances are overwhelming that the Negro family will live in a segregated area or a new transition area that will soon become segregated—a slum or a housing project for low-income groups; and an upgraded all-Negro development, or fringe area for middle- and upper-income groups. And the chances are overwhelming that the Negro family will be paying premium prices for the housing it has.

The Negro family has become increasingly self-conscious and anxious about housing. This development is related not only to scarcity, lack of free choice, and neighborhood and community tensions, but also to changes in comfort, success, and status models. Added to the heightened family and personal value of decent housing and good neighborhoods as proper settings for child-rearing and family living, is the increased importance of housing as a status symbol and measure of mobility. This is, of course, a value that the Negro family shares with all American families. For the Negro family there is additional emphasis—and therefore added possibilities of frustration—because of what housing means now as an overt demonstration of achievement and worth to both the Negro and white communities.

The problem of public school education is directly related

to, and aggravated by, the housing situation for Negroes, particularly in urban communities; and it is marked by similar values, needs, and anxieties among the Negro families. Because of the residential concentration of Negro families in the central and older parts of the city, a high proportion of Negro public school pupils are in older, overcrowded school buildings that tend to be segregated in fact, if not in law. The effects on the family are direct not only in terms of the quality of the education of the child but also in terms of the anxieties and resentments this situation arouses in Negro parents of the stable working class and middle class. The effects are the more acute because of the high values placed on education as a means of advancement in all levels of the Negro community; of the effect of the Supreme Court decision and desegregation in the South, which spotlight and make more onerous segregated schooling in the North; and because of the great current public concern over the quality of public education.

Negro families, and organizations representing them, are showing increased sensitivity over what are perceived as any competitive disadvantages their children have, for whatever reasons. Negro family heads are likely to be concerned not just about the availability of schooling as such, but about the quality of education available to their children and the characteristics of particular schools. For the second successive year a group of Negro parents in New York City are refusing to send their children to what they describe as an inferior, overcrowded school.

The added value placed on education of children as a

means of escaping low and achieving higher status is a myth-like cultural theme. It induces anxiety on all levels. The "compensatory projection of parental ambition" onto children in middle-class, white-collar Negro families is expected and understood; however, Merton points out that "in a recent research on the social organization of public housing developments, we have found among both Negroes and whites in lower occupational levels, a substantial proportion having aspirations for a professional career for their children." Reiss and Rhodes, in a Nashville study, found that "Negroes require a somewhat higher level of educational attainment than the general population and place a substantially greater value on schooling than do whites."

If, as Merton suggests, the "syndrome of lofty aspirations and limited realistic opportunities . . . is precisely the pattern which invites deviant behavior," [3] the conclusions of Reiss and Rhodes provide an important clue to reasons why, and ways in which, Negro mothers might prime both achievement and deviant behavior in children:

White mothers in the lower stratum of American society are less likely than Negro mothers to project high aspirations on to their children if they are low rather than high I.Q. children. . . . [We] suggest that the importance of schooling to the Negro family makes their members more likely than those of the white family to project unrealistic educational goals in the low I.Q. child. There is only a small race difference in subjects' educational aspirations such that Negroes are somewhat more likely to aspire toward a college education.[4]

[3] Robert K. Merton, *Social Theory and Social Structure*, Revised and Enlarged Edition (Glencoe: Free Press, 1957), p. 159.
[4] Albert J. Reiss, Jr. and Albert L. Rhodes, "Are Educational Norms

The absolute chances of Negro youths for higher education are increasing: In 1950 more Negroes graduated from college than had graduated from high school in 1920. The rate of increase of Negro college enrollment during that period was six times that of whites. The fact that slightly better than 1 in 10 Negro families include an adult with some college education in contrast to slightly more than 1 in 4 white families, shows a sizeable gap still. Further, as suggested earlier, general anxiety about education is likely to make Negro families more concerned and anxious about the educational future and prospects of children. And all the more so when the increased costs of education are juxtaposed to the generally low income of the Negro family.

One of the most persistent and popular stereotypes is that lower-class parents have little or no interest in the education of their children. Refutation and an indication of the need to examine other factors are furnished in a study made in a New York school with a pupil population predominately Puerto Rican and Negro. A field worker was assigned to work with the parents. The results:

A year and a half later there were forty-five Negro and Puerto Rican mothers working on the Executive and seven other committees that formed the leadership core of the PTA; the Executive Committee of fifteen Negro and Puerto Rican mothers had felt confident enough to visit the superintendent of all the elementary schools and make a request in non-hostile terms; a parent chorus was giving concerts in schools; the PTA had compiled and mimeographed a directory of available health services

and Goals of Conforming, Truant, and Delinquent Adolescents Influenced by Group Position in American Society?" *Journal of Negro Education*, Vol. XXVIII (Summer, 1959), pp. 258, 261.

and had set up a polio clinic for the neighborhood; and one of the mothers, a Negro, had become president of the Community Health Committee. These parents, who had seemed to take no interest in their children's education, proved that, although oppressed with problems of living conditions, health, and economic security, they were deeply concerned with their school and had the capacity for positive action and leadership.[5]

The foregoing suggests the heavy impact now of housing and schooling values and anxieties as factors affecting one aspect of child rearing and the roles of adults. However, the ways in which, and the relative success with which, Negro families carry out these functions, are primarily related to family size and structure and class position.

During the past generation, the decline in the average size of Negro households has been much less than that of white households, due to differences in the birth rate and in the practice and necessity of doubling. Negro households are significantly larger, containing on the average more children and more adults. Since 1950, the number of Negro households has been increasing at a rate more than twice that for white households. And Negroes have a relatively larger proportion of both small and large households. This is related to the large proportion of childless women, the high proportion of women with large numbers of children, and the high proportion of lodgers.

The chances continue disproportionately high that much of the socialization of the Negro child will take place in a household headed by a woman, not headed by both or either

[5] John H. Niemeyer, "Splitting the Social Atom," *Saturday Review*, September 12, 1959, p. 18.

of his own parents, with relatives other than his own parents and brothers and sisters, or with nonrelatives, and with direct support or subsidy from public funds.

Since the conventional and stable type of family or household is not the instrument of socialization for many children, or of community-orientation and status-giving for many adults, it is probable that persons, institutions, and experiences outside of the family or household are relatively more important, and make their influence felt earlier, in the Negro family. And the relatively larger role played by nonfamily factors in socialization in the Negro community probably applies on all levels and for all family types. Evidence supporting this is found in one of the few recent examples of a follow-up study of Negro family functions. In 1953–56 John H. Rohrer and his associates in New Orleans did a follow-up investigation of the adolescent subjects used in Allison Davis' and John Dollard's 1937–38 study published as *Children of Bondage*. They studied "group patterning of primary social identification" in child training in a class-stratified sample of Negro women householders as well as among the original subjects of the Davis-Dollard study. Their study "failed to reveal that there was any universal systematic training given in caste etiquette, at least before school age." [6]

All that this finding suggests, however, is that the Negro child probably gets most of his racial training by absorbing

[6] John H. Rohrer, "Sociocultural Factors in Personality Development," National Conference on Social Welfare, *The Social Welfare Forum, Official Proceedings, Philadelphia,* 1957 (New York: Columbia University Press, 1957), p. 195.

informally and unsystematically clues and cues from members of the household and from outside the family. Merton points out: "Nor is the socialization confined to direct training and disciplining. The process is, at least in part, inadvertent . . . Not infrequently, *children detect and incorporate cultural uniformities even when these remain implicit and have not been reduced to rules."* [7]

Edward K. Weaver asked children at an elementary school in the South to write answers to the question "When did you first discover that you were a Negro?" In only three of the thirty replies cited as "typical" did a child report the first explicit revelation as having come from direct family instruction or from inside the home. And in these instances it was the grandparent who gave the instruction or warning.[8]

Statistics continue to confirm the classic pictures of disorganization, dependency, and inadequacy, and larger proportions of broken families and female heads. However, we have little or no recent data to tell us what these facts and forms mean and represent in the present context. It may be that the classic explanations are still valid, but we cannot be sure, and there is a risk in assuming or guessing, without the facts that go beyond the statistics and older studies.

The proportion of Negroes married but living apart from spouses is three to four times higher than that of whites. Approximately 1 in 9 Negro married women and 1 in 12 Negro married men are living apart from their spouses. Ne-

[7] Merton, *Social Theory,* p. 158.
[8] Edward K. Weaver, "Racial Sensitivity Among Negro Children," *Phylon,* Vol. XVII (First Quarter, 1956), pp. 52–60.

groes constitute about 1 in 11 of all families in the United States, 1 in 14 of all husband-wife families, and 1 in 5 of all families with female heads.

Much of the incidence of these and the related characteristics is, of course, explained, as Frazier has done so effectively, by the persistence of rural-folk traditions and ways in interaction with urban, secular imperatives. However, not enough is known about the dynamics of present family forms and functions and about the behavior patterns which are distinctly urban products with a dynamic and history of their own. The forms, as in the case of the family headed by the female, may be the same but the context in which they fit and function has probably changed in important details. Knowledge of background and of a tradition, which itself is changing, are necessary but probably not sufficient to explain and understand the Negro family, particularly in the changing cities of today.

In this connection, it is probable that even the time-honored reference to desertion as "the poor man's divorce" needs closer examination and discrimination, although it is abundantly clear that the racial difference in desertion remains very significant. In a study made in Philadelphia, Kephart found that "when the bottom three occupational classes are combined . . . for the whites these classes are slightly overrepresented in desertions, while among Negroes, surprisingly, these classes are slightly underrepresented. . . . [Among] the Negroes the greatest overrepresentation is found in the semiskilled category." He suggests as explanatory factors possible underreporting because of ignorance of the law and the "lingering tradition" among Negro lower classes—the wives may not want husbands back. Balancing these, however, he adds, is the fact that lower-class wives must have family support and cannot get public assistance unless the husband is reported.[9]

The census data indicate that "color is a differential in marriage impermanence only in separation and widowhood." Divorce rates for Negro women tend to rise as education rises up to, but not including, college graduation.

Increases in illegitimacy rates among Negroes and in the proportion participating in the Aid to Dependent Children program are associated with recent increases in urbanization. For the general population, the number of births to unmarried mothers has been rising at a faster rate than births to married mothers. The illegitimacy rate in 1956 was 46.5 per 1,000 live births as compared with 37.9 per 1,000 live births in 1940. Teen-agers contributed nearly half the number of illegitimacies in 1940, and 40 percent in 1956. The predominant part of the increase between 1940 and 1955 is to be accounted for by nonwhite illegitimate births, which increased at a rate more than twice that for whites. There has been a tendency for the nonwhite rate to be higher in Northern urban centers than the estimated nonwhite percentage for the entire country including the Southern states. It is undoubtedly true now as Frazier points out that "illegitimacy, like other forms of family disorganization, tends to become segregated in the poorer sections of the Negro

[9] William M. Kephart, "Occupational Level and Marital Disruption," *American Sociological Review*, Vol. 20 (August, 1955).

community located in the slum areas of our cities." The fact that illegitimacy rates are increasing in urban areas at the same time that the general economic and educational level of the Negro population is improving may reflect a short-run rise attributable in the main to the disorganization related to the rapid influx and piling up of low-income groups. There are certainly other factors operating currently about which we know little, which are independent of race.

Another measure of family inadequacy or disorganization closely associated with increasing urbanization of the Negro is the rate of participation in the Aid to Dependent Children program. This is not surprising inasmuch as the family crises leading to need for ADC (absence or incapacity of father) occur relatively more frequently among low-income groups. Urbanization of ADC recipients is increasing, particularly among Negroes who make up an increasing portion of the ADC load—31 percent in 1948; 40 percent in 1956. More than one-half of the nonwhite family recipients live in cities of over 50,000 population; nearly two-thirds of the Negro recipients are in metropolitan counties. The overrepresentation of Negro families on ADC rolls is a political and administrative issue in both many Southern states and Northern communities with large concentrations of Negroes. This is another example of the acutely "political" character of the needs and rights of disadvantaged Negroes.

The increase, and the differential, in the labor force participation of Negro wives reflect different values and pressure among them: the greater need to work to maintain or supplement a basically low family income, particularly among lower occupational and educational levels; increased incentive or wish to work, in order to improve or maintain a desired level of living, particularly among mobile, better-educated, middle-class families; and possibly, more favorable conditions for leaving children with relatives or others. The significance of this last is questionable, particularly among low-income newcomers to the large cities. Social workers report an increase in "door-key children" and an acute current shortage of low-cost nursery care in impoverished urban areas.

Negro wives in just over two-fifths of all Negro husband-wife families work; about half of those with no children under six work; and nearly 1 in 4 of those with children under six is in the labor force. The mothers of children under six are less than half as likely to be working as other mothers, regardless of race and other variables. And the differences in labor force participation of mothers, Negro and white, who share family responsibilities with a husband and those who are themselves the head of the family, as in the case of a disproportionate number of Negroes, are growing less. That this does not imply the same values and pressures is indicated by the fact that the income level of nearly one-half the broken families with female heads is below $2,000. There is some convergence in the employment rates of Negro and white wives, but the differences remain large.

Class Changes

The heavy wave of professional concern and popular preoccupation with social class values, tastes, and behavior has had telling and, on the whole, favorable effects on the Negro community and the Negro family. One result has been the casting up for popular recognition of features of the Negro community which had been blurred, ignored, not too well understood, and attributed to color. First came the necessary assumption and then the recognition and acceptance that there are class differences within the Negro community. As a result, the Negro's self-esteem and aspirations have received a decisive boost. The impact of the idea, and the demonstration of class in the Negro community have now done what the old, poignant protest, "All Negroes are not alike!" could not do. Applying the class approach to the Negro has helped the public to enlarge and correct its image of the Negro, and it has provided a new, nonthreatening basis for discrimination. It improves the chances of identification, communication, and contact; and it tends to cut across or transcend racial lines. Now, one pauses and asks, "Is this a class or a race trait?"

Very American, and "hopeful" for all concerned, is the assumption that better education and better jobs help more Negroes to acquire middle-class characteristics. For the American middle-class mind, the fewer lower-class Negroes, or Negroes with lower-class characteristics, the less the threat and the cost of disorganization and dependency associated with Negroes. For middle-class Negroes and their families, the fewer Negroes with lower-class characteristics, the less the threat to their own status is the old custom of lumping all Negroes, and the better the chance to work out with minimum anxiety just who they are and with whom they identify.

In addition to what has been said above about the class concept as a catalyst of favorable change it should be pointed out that some of the assumptions and clichés with respect to class values and behavior, particularly lower-class, are among the factors that deter better understanding and policy-making. Using any of the usual socio-economic indices, proportionately more Negro families are in the lower-class. Although it is probably true, this fact alone does not mean necessarily that proportionately fewer Negroes adhere to middle-class values or aspire to middle-class goals. The Negro family's generally low socio-economic status, and discrimination, affect the chances to afford, cultivate, and enjoy some of the American middle-class success values—education, respectability, thrift, etc.; however, the appreciation and grasp of these is another matter. The force of education as a value on all levels of the Negro community has already been discussed.

Among the lower-income or working class Negro families, there have been some postwar changes in income and education, and increased exposure to and absorption of mass culture through the press, radio, and television. These have altered images, aspirations, and practices—and conspicuously along lines of consumption and leisure time. Probably not at the same rate, but certainly along with the rest of America, the Negro family is undergoing an upgrading of tastes and of its ability to satisfy them. This "deproletarianization" of the working class, and the rise and spread of the Negro middle-class tend to make class and ethnic differences less significant and less invidious. Of course, there will be lags and resistant ethnic and class strongholds—but all of the pressures, both outside the Negro community and within it, are enhancing the ability and the opportunity to conform in essentials to middle-class American ways. The desire and design for conformity, even "over-conformity," the American Negro has always had, and the results at times seem to border on caricature as Frazier points out in his portrait of the middle class in *Black Bourgeoisie* (1957).

The force of class changes and the diffusion of middle-class standards and ways shows up not only in the consumption behavior of the Negro family, as in automobiles, housing, dress, etc., but more importantly in child-rearing and family roles.

Davis and Havighurst concluded, in their influential study made in 1943, that "there are *cultural differences* in the personality formation of middle-class compared with lower-class people, *regardless of color,* due to their early training. And for the same reason there should be further but less marked cultural differences between Negroes and whites of the same social class." [10] The logic of events and some evidence since 1943 would indicate that some convergence has occurred with respect to the influence of both class and color factors in child-rearing, if regional differences are held constant. In a recent review of research in this area Bronfenbrenner compared "the traditional view of the differences between the middle- and lower-class styles of life, as docu-

[10] Allison Davis and Robert J. Havighurst, "Social Class and Color Differences in Child-Rearing" in Guy E. Swanson, T. M. Newcomb, E. L. Hartley, and others, *Readings in Social Psychology,* Revised Edition (New York: Holt, 1952), p. 550.

mented in the classic descriptions of Warner, Davis, Dollard, and . . . Spinley, Clausen, and Miller and Swanson." He concluded: "To the extent that our data even approach this picture, it is for the period before World War II rather than for the present-day. . . . As for the lower-class the fit is far better for the actual behavior of the parents than for the values they seek to instill in their children." [11]

Since, beyond the social class factor, "child-rearing practices are likely to change most quickly in those segments of society which have closest access and are most receptive to the agencies or agents of change," it is probably true that the Negro family as a category, like the rural family as a category, lags in the rate and extent of change in child-rearing practices.

Clues to some of the dynamics of lag as well as those of change are to be found in the differences in adoption practices between the Negro community and the white community, and in the efforts to encourage change in the Negro family's practices. Among the reasons suggested as affecting adoption behavior are these: many Negro couples come from or live in areas where adoptive facilities are not developed or not available; fear of rejection; limited income and inadequate housing. Special agency and community programs in Chicago, New York, Los Angeles, and San Francisco represent the first organized efforts on a significant scale to solve this program.

Such efforts are similar to those established or proposed to change other practices or circumstances affecting Negro

[11] Uri Bronfenbrenner, "Socialization and Social Class Through Time and Space," in E. E. Macoby, T. M. Newcomb, and E. L. Hartley, *Readings in Social Psychology* (New York: Holt, 1958), pp. 400–25.

family life. They reflect public and professional awareness of the threat and social costs involved as well as increasing recognition that such nonmiddle-class behavior is a result of neither inherent racial nor immutable class characteristics. They show the desire, if not the "need," to grant middle-class potentialities to Negro families; and, frequently, to implement their attainment—both under segregated and unsegregated conditions—with public and private funds.

Notable changes in the roles of Negro family members are due to class mobility and the resulting closer adherence to prevailing American sex role patterns, as well as to the gains and dilemmas of desegregation. For well-known reasons, the influence of the Negro woman in the Negro family has been very strong. It is likely to continue strong in different segments of the Negro community but for different reasons. The reasons with respect to the low-income working class family that is broken are clear, and they will continue to operate. In the mobile or middle-class family the influence of the woman becomes stronger because parents in this type of Negro family tend to be sensitive to the same images, if not precisely the identical pressures, related to the organization and values of present-day business life and the rituals of status, notably place and style of living, that affect their white prototype. And as Frazier points out, the pressures may actually be stronger. Although influence of the Negro woman is increasing, there are gains or changes for the male parent, also. Job, salary, and educational improvement tend to increase confidence and permit him to play and to see himself in the part of the more conventional wage-earner, husband, parent, and participant in community affairs.

In his *Black Bourgeoisie*, Frazier suggests that "In the South the middle-class Negro male is not only prevented from playing a masculine role, but generally he must let Negro women assume leadership in any show of militancy." [12] This is probably less true now—though how much less, we do not know—than it was ten years ago, and than it will be ten years from now, yet dramatic changes are not to be expected. Although it is still "safer" for women—both Negro and white—to act in a strong manner in matters affecting race relations in the South, there are differences between what it is "safe" for the male to do in the cities of the South today and what it is "safe" to do in rural areas. Even here it should be pointed out that with few exceptions in both urban and rural areas, the leadership for recent moves challenging segregation has come mainly from business and professional groups—ministers, lawyers, insurance men, and in many instances medical practitioners—who have been protected by their relative independence from direct economic pressure. And they have been able to use most effectively the support and technical assistance of national organizations as well as their own local strategic political power. These situations have provided new opportunities for the male to play a more positive role; and they have provided models and images for other Negro males. One of the reasons why more males are

[12] E. Franklin Frazier, *Black Bourgeoisie* (Glencoe: Free Press, 1957), p. 221.

not militant or under severe pressure to be so is that much of the struggle for rights does not involve person-to-person conflict or the need for direct confrontation. Important aspects of the struggle are waged by organizations which in this sense are surrogates that relieve the direct pressure on the individual. The demand and real need is for Negro families to supply and support the local innovator who will make the initial challenge. In Montgomery, this part was played by Mrs. Rosa Parks; at the University of Alabama by Miss Lucy; in Little Rock by Mrs. Bates (effectively backed by Mr. Bates, and other men), and notably by the female students (Minnie Jean Brown, Elizabeth Eckford, et al.); and in New York City by the mothers of Harlem school children.

The family role and the community position of the average Negro male, in contrast to the average white male, are affected in direct and subtle ways by the continuing differences in the following: the industry in which the Negro husband and father works, the job level or area, the earnings associated with it, the degree of certainty he has with respect to maintaining it and the chances of advancement he sees in it, and dependence on wages—in contrast to salary, commissions, profits, investments.

Since the job is a crucial determinant of where and how the family fits in the society, and of the effectiveness of its claim on many of the society's rewards, probably the most important single clue to the quality of change in the Negro family and in the Negro community is found in the job picture, particularly for the male. In this sense, then, any recent improvements in that picture as a result of increasing desegregation and urbanization represent the most solid and significant of recent gains for the Negro family. And continued changes in the employment picture are necessary to underwrite in practical terms the salutary changes in self-conceptions, movement, participation, and tastes that have recently come rapidly to the Negro family.

A HEALTHIER WORLD

by GEORGE ROSEN, M.D.

IT IS almost impossible to overemphasize the effect the development of microbiology and immunology have had on the health of the community. Action in the interest of community health today comprises an intricate maze of activities involving the services and energies of a wide variety of professional and lay people. Much of this work stems from the application of bacteriological and immunological knowledge to the actual problems of disease control.

Public health departments, as set up in the nineteenth century, were concerned essentially with the control of contagious diseases through environmental sanitation. However, as the microorganisms responsible for specific diseases were identified and their mode of action uncovered, the way was opened for the control of infectious diseases on a more rational, accurate, and specific basis. Such activity by public health authorities became possible on an unprecedented scale. The first decade of the twentieth century saw a solid basis for the control of a number of infectious diseases, and

George Rosen, M.D. is Professor of Public Health Education at the School of Public Health and Administrative Medicine of Columbia University.

throughout succeeding decades advances along this line have continued with increasing tempo.

The meaning of this trend is clearly evident in the case of diphtheria. By 1900, diphtheria could be diagnosed by precise bacteriological methods; the sick person could be treated with diphtheria antitoxin, and well carriers could be detected, thus making possible effective control. The next important step was the direct prevention of the disease by active immunization, a method developed logically from earlier knowledge on the use of diphtheria antitoxin as a passive immunizing agent as well as a therapeutic agent. By 1920 knowledge and tools were available for a full-scale mass attack on diphtheria. In that year active immunization of school children began, and by 1940 the disease had been virtually eliminated as a cause of death: the mortality rate of diphtheria was 1.1 per 100,000 in 1940, in striking contrast to the rate of 785 per 100,000 which obtained in 1894.

The drop in diphtheria morbidity and mortality was not due to preventive immunization alone. This rapid decline actually began in the nineteenth century before diphtheria antitoxin was generally used, and continued progressively even before preventive immunization became widespread. Nor was the decline of diphtheria an isolated instance of the control of disease. Many other major infectious diseases had begun to wane before the full effects of the bacteriological discoveries made themselves felt. Beginning about 1870, there was a continuing downward trend in deaths from such diseases as yellow fever, smallpox, typhoid and typhus fevers, malaria, and tuberculosis. These developments undoubtedly reflect in part the impact of the sanitary reform movement of the nineteenth century. Acting on the theory that a clean city is a healthy city, city governmental and private agencies sought to clean up the physical environment, and made efforts to provide unadulterated food and clean water; in short, action was taken to provide decent living conditions.

Yet, whatever factors were involved in the decline of specific infectious diseases, we must note that children were the chief beneficiaries. The degree of benefit obtained from measures taken for the improvement of milk and water is clearly shown by the trend of the infant mortality rate in New York City. In 1885 the infant death rate was 273 per 1,000 live births; by 1915 it had dropped sharply to 94 per 1,000. Equally beneficial results were obtained through the widespread adoption of smallpox vaccination after 1870. Children also benefited from a decline in the virulence of scarlet fever.

This brief account of the decline in specific infectious diseases and its significance for child health need not be pursued in detail. What it meant in simple quantitative terms can be seen from the following estimates. According to W. S. Thompson, the probable number of survivors to age sixty-five from 1,000 births in the United States increased from 325 in 1875 to 695 in 1940.

While communicable diseases were increasingly being brought under control, and action was being taken for more effective sanitation, new developments occurred during the first decade of the twentieth century which vastly broadened the horizons of public health workers and turned their attention to new tasks. Surveying the community with a critical eye, some of those engaged in health and social work were not entirely satisfied with what they saw. Investigations of the poorer classes of the community showed that their health and environment were highly unsatisfactory. Malnutrition was rife, maternal mortality was high, and while infant mortality had declined, the health of children attending school as well as that of preschool children was found to be extremely poor.

On the basis of these findings, socially minded citizens, physicians, clergymen, social workers, and government officials concerned themselves with all phases of child life. This movement to improve the health and welfare of children was directed at first toward reducing the high child mortality rate. Experts recognized that a large part of infant mortality was preventable—that it was caused by malnourishment, parental ignorance, contaminated food, and other factors attributable entirely or in part to poverty. Some of these factors were remediable, while the effects of others might be greatly lessened. Since the problem had many ramifications, it was attacked along a number of different lines: by instructing mothers in the proper feeding and care of children; through the provision of clean milk; through legislation regulating the work of expectant mothers; and by providing facilities for the care of babies of working mothers.

These endeavors to improve child health were a characteristic and prominent feature of the larger movement for social reform and the amelioration of poor health conditions which marked the United States during the two decades preceding

its entry into World War I. The orientation of this movement was empirical and pragmatic; its proponents had confidence in what might be accomplished by conscious social
action. In varying degrees the same phenomenon could be
found in other countries at this time, and it is evident that
this was a response to the problems thrown up by an advancing industrialization accompanied by urban expansion.
Protest and affirmation, vigorous discontent and abounding
confidence in constructive social endeavor led to action in
various directions.

The beginnings of child welfare efforts at the turn of the
century followed the same general lines in both European
and American urban communities. At first, stations were set
up to provide clean milk; later these became well-child stations where the health of infants and young children was
supervised, and mothers were instructed in the care of the
child at home. It was known that the diarrhea from which
so many babies younger than two years of age died, especially
in the summer, was due largely to unsafe, highly contaminated milk. It was also known that the mortality among
breast-fed babies was considerably lower than among those
artificially fed. Consequently, the prime objective of all those
concerned with infant health was to encourage breast feeding or, when this was not possible, to provide a safe and
effective substitute.

There was yet, however, little or no emphasis on community responsibility for the promotion of child health.
During the nineteenth century there were sporadic efforts in

Europe and the United States towards this end, but it was not until the turn of the century that facilities and programs for infant and child care began to appear in rapid succession. In 1889, an American physician, Henry Koplik (1858–1927), established a "milk station," which was actually a very simple consultation center for mothers and children, at the Good Samaritan Dispensary in New York. However, demonstrations initiated in France along these lines exerted a wide effect in other countries. Most important was the work of Pierre Budin, who established a pioneer system of infant consultation centers, which served as a model for other countries.

In these efforts it was recognized that mothers who could not breast-feed their babies should be able to obtain clean cow's milk at a reasonable price. This concept first took hold in France, and milk stations, known as *gouettes de lait*, were set up in Paris. This example was soon followed in New York City by the philanthropist Nathan Strauss, who was interested in health problems. In 1893, he began to set up a system of milk stations which was widely copied and which he supported for twenty-six years until 1919. The milk was modified according to formula, pasteurized, and dispensed in nursing bottles, and mothers were instructed in feeding their babies. In 1902, these stations distributed 250,000 bottles monthly.

The Strauss milk stations provided the impetus for governmental action along these lines in the United States. Set up under health department auspices, experiments in child feeding were carried on, pasteurized milk was distributed at cost, and mothers were instructed in the proper care and feeding of infants.

Provision of clean milk, teaching mothers to care for their babies, and creation of clinics where this could be done properly were the three basic elements that entered into the development of well-child services. Toward the end of the first decade of the twentieth century, a number of private and governmental agencies in various countries had already demonstrated what might be accomplished along each of these avenues in promoting child health. Recognition that the execution of these activities as a total program was a community responsibility to be borne by the agency officially concerned with the health of the community was first achieved in New York City.

The establishment in 1908 of a Division of Child Hygiene in the New York City Health Department is a landmark in the history of child health work. This unit was the first of its kind in the world and was to set a pattern for other health departments in the United States and abroad. S. Josephine Baker, a physician who had been a child health inspector in the Department, was put in charge. Early in the summer of 1908, she had shown how infant deaths could be greatly reduced through prevention of disease. In a congested section of New York's lower East Side the name and address of every newborn baby in the district was obtained from the registrar of records the day after its birth. On that day, a public health nurse visited the mother and taught her how to keep the baby well. When the results were tabulated after about two months, it was found that there were 1,200 fewer deaths in the district than there had been in the preceding summer during the same period. This demonstration of how to give babies a healthy start in life provided the basis for the work of the division.

One of its first achievements was to employ milk distribution as a way of coming into contact with mothers to teach them proper child care. Attention was also directed to the health of babies in foundling hospitals and to children of school age. Long before the idea of maternal deprivation was conceived, Josephine Baker pointed out that good hygienic conditions during pregnancy were fundamental to the health of babies. Similarly, before the term "health education" was invented, the educational process was being employed as a fundamental tool in the campaign to save infant life. An instance in point is the development of the Little Mothers' League. Recognizing that the "little mother," that is, the little girl in a poor family who has to take care of younger children because her mother works, was an important factor in infant deaths, Dr. Baker organized a flock of Little Mothers' Leagues among school girls. These children were given practical instruction in child care and served as missionaries of the new gospel in tenements and slums.

The Division of Child Hygiene represented one avenue of attack on the preventable deaths of children. However, this was a battle waged simultaneously on many fronts. As we have seen, of outstanding importance was the provision of clean milk. In 1901, W. H. Park of the New York City Bacteriological Laboratory showed that milk delivered to customers in the summer was generally highly contaminated with bacteria and might contain more than 5,000,000 organisms per cubic centimeter. The following year, together with L. Emmett Holt, he addressed himself to the problem of infantile diarrhea and its relation to the bacteriology of the milk consumed. The results clearly showed that the quality of milk fed to infants during hot weather influenced the amount of illness to which they were subject and their mortality.

In 1910, the New York City Board of Health began to require that all milk used for drinking purposes be properly pasteurized, and two years later the Board adopted a grading system and standards for all milk brought into the city for sale. Clean milk became available for New York's babies, rich and poor. The degree to which infants benefited by the measures is indicated by the virtual elimination of deaths from summer diarrhea. By 1923, scarcely a vestige remained of the great rise in infant mortality that generally came with the hot weather.

The beginnings of official action on behalf of child health in New York City have been described in some detail because they illustrate the elements and interrelationships that entered into the development of this field of health action in the United States. What New York City had done on a local level was carried forward by the states and the federal government. Federal recognition was accorded to the field of child health when President Taft, on April 9, 1912, signed a bill creating a Children's Bureau which was charged with investigating and reporting "upon all matters pertaining to the welfare of children and child life among all classes of our people."

The idea for such a Bureau came from Florence Kelley and Lillian Wald, both members of that dedicated, militant group of men and women who at the end of the nineteenth century and during the first quarter of the present century undertook to curb some of the worst abuses created by industrialization and who prepared the way for the social legislation we take for granted today. Its initial appropriation was only $26,640, and the Bureau wisely devoted much of its activity to a reconnaissance of the field assigned to it by Congress. Much of the data collected before the 1930s provided a solid basis of fact for later federal action in the interest of mothers and children.

That infancy could not be protected without the protection of maternity was one of the principles on which the Children's Bureau developed its program. In the United States, the first organized program of health care during the prenatal period was provided in 1908 by the Pediatric Department of the New York Outdoor Medical Clinic. Visiting nurse service for pregnant women in their homes followed a year later in Boston, under the sponsorship of the Women's Municipal League. In 1912 such services were initiated in St. Louis. Initially, the Children's Bureau participated in the field of maternal health by studying maternal mortality, and by providing instruction for mothers. For the latter purpose, the Bureau, in 1913, published a pamphlet entitled *Prenatal Care*, which has been a best-seller ever since.

Since then, great strides have been taken in maternity care

in the United States. These have gone hand in hand with and are in part the result of important social and scientific developments. For example, in 1935, 63 percent of all babies were born in places other than hospitals, and 13 percent of all live births were not attended by physicians. By 1956, almost 95 percent of all babies born in this country were delivered in hospitals, and 97 percent of all registered births were attended by physicians. Increased public awareness of the value of maternity care coupled with advances in medical knowledge have been responsible for the sharp declines in the mortality of mothers and infants over the past thirty years, and the general improvement in their health. While there still are areas and groups in the United States—chiefly rural, low income, and of lower-than-average educational level—that do not fully enjoy these benefits, even these have shown improvement in recent years.

To a very considerable degree, this is a result of action by the federal government. During and after World War I developments in the care of mothers and children came rapidly, especially with the passage of the Maternity and Infancy (Sheppard-Towner) Act in 1921. Through the extension of grants-in-aid to private and public agencies, a strong stimulus was given to prenatal care and child welfare work. For seven years, a successful program based on federal-state cooperation was carried on, but in 1929 it failed to secure further appropriations from Congress. Six years later, however, it was reenacted on a much more ambitious scale as Title V of the Social Security Act. This section authorized grants to be made each year to the various states through the

Children's Bureau to help them extend and improve their maternal and child health services, as well as services for handicapped children.

During World War II, the Children's Bureau also administered through state agencies a vast emergency program of infant and maternity care for the wives of service men. By holding unswervingly to a broad conception of child welfare as concerned with all the social aspects of child life, by insisting on the use of qualified personnel in all programs, and by encouraging communities to develop programs on the local and state levels to improve the health and welfare of mothers and children, the Children's Bureau has played a leading role in developing these aspects of community health in the United States.

Action in the interest of mothers and infants during the past half-century was paralleled by the development of health services for school children. Medical examination of school children was initiated to control contagion. Much of the early work in this field was sketchy. It was simply a crude attempt to screen out the worst cases of infectious diseases, though many minor ones could be brought to light by physicians who were conscientious and experienced. After a while, however, it was recognized that this was not enough. In addition to such diseases as diphtheria, measles, and scarlet fever, school children in large urban centers, especially in slum areas, suffered from skin diseases (pediculosis, scabies, ringworm, impetigo), eye conditions (trachoma), malnutrition, and physical defects. It was recognized that education of parent and child was necessary to combat these conditions.

An effective method of dealing with the situation was first developed in New York City. In 1902, at the request of the Health Commissioner, Lillian Wald of the Henry Street Settlement loaned one of her best qualified nurses to carry out a pilot demonstration in a particularly bad school. After a few months, this nurse had evolved an educational approach that was effective in checking the minor infections. In consequence, she was appointed as the first full-time school nurse in the United States, and soon additional nurses were employed to work along the lines she had developed. This approach was eminently successful and contributed in large measure to the eventual disappearance of many of the conditions listed above.

With the passage of time, many changes have taken place in the provision of health services for school children. There has been a shift of emphasis from the initial limited objectives to a broader concept of the field of school health. From a concern with the control of contagion had come the introduction of public health nursing in schools. The program was then expanded by the introduction of periodic medical examinations and follow-up procedures for the correction of discovered physical defects. Once interest in the health problems of children was aroused in the United States developments occurred in a number of other directions.

The school lunch movement had its inception in New York in 1908 as an effort to supplement the diet of undernourished children. Philadelphia, Chicago, and other large cities followed the lead of New York in the supplementary feeding of poor children. Originally, the program provided a warm lunch for children whose parents found it inconvenient to have them come home. The need for further work in this field was underscored by Dr. Josephine Baker who in 1917 estimated that 21 percent of the children in the New York schools were undernourished. In 1918, Dr. Thomas Wood estimated that this was true of 15 to 25 percent of the school children in the United States.

The most important single factor in developing the school lunch program was the depression of the 1930s. Following its reorganization in 1935, the Federal Surplus Commodities Corporation undertook an active program of reducing agricultural surpluses. One phase of this work was the school lunch program. At the end of 1938, forty-five states and the District of Columbia were participating in the program, and over a period of five years of operation about 130,000,000 meals were served. There is no doubt that this program was of direct benefit in improving children's health. At the same time, emphasis was also put on nutrition education, a subject that had been introduced into the school curriculum in 1918, and has since become a regular part of both elementary and secondary education. The lunch program was formalized in the National School Lunch Act of 1946, which provided grants-in-aid to states for school lunch programs. This Act was important in stimulating the further development of such programs throughout the United States.

Free clinics for school children were established in 1912 in New York City, as a service of the municipal health department. These included a general medical clinic, a skin clinic, an eye clinic, and a tonsil and adenoid clinic. Similar facilities have been established by many other communities. Today, they may include dental clinics, mental hygiene clinics, as well as clinics for cardiacs and other handicapped children.

Dental health service got off to a slow start in the United States. Only since the 1930s has there been a broad development of active programs. The growth in public health programs since then is indicated by the organization in 1938 of the American Association of Public Health Dentists. Since 1948, the fluoridation of community water supplies promises to reduce considerably the burden of dental care in the school-age population.

It is manifestly impossible to develop in detail all the trends in school health work. One tendency, however, should be noted. Beginning in the 1920s and continuing into the 1930s, health workers and educators began to question the methods of school health work. It was felt that a hurried routine examination of a child without parent present and with little attention to follow-up procedures was a sterile activity. To break out of this web of routine and to develop better means of providing health care, a number of studies were undertaken, beginning with that launched in 1923 by the American Child Health Association. Eventually, in July, 1936, the Astoria Health District Study was initiated in New York City and carried on for four years.

Much of what has happened since then in the administration and practice of school health work is based on the Astoria demonstration and its results. Today, greater emphasis is placed on more adequate, though possibly less frequent, medical examinations by the family physician or the school physician. Teacher-nurse conferences on suspected health problems and special examinations by the school doctor are being used to see that children most urgently in need of care receive it.

Nevertheless a more fully effective school health service in the United States is still a goal to be attained. One obstacle is the division of responsibility that exists in many communities between educational and health authorities in the administration of health services for school children. A second is the frequently unclear and truncated role of the school physician, who screens and diagnoses but does not treat, and his relation to the family doctor when a family has one. Thirdly, the family must work with teacher, doctor, and nurse to give the child the care he needs, and this as we are only too well aware is dependent in considerable degree on economic, social, and cultural factors. In short, as long as the care of the "total" child is divided among several agencies and a variety of personnel, often inadequate in some respect, one cannot expect the full benefits of school health work.

Yet, despite inadequacies and defects still to be found in the health of the American people, the past fifty years have witnessed an unprecedented overall trend toward the improvement of community health. This advance, however, has not been uniform either within communities or among various parts of the world. A large group of countries generally underdeveloped in an economic and technological sense, and often new as independent nations, still have problems of preventable disease like those with which the countries of western Europe and the United States had to cope three-quarters of a century ago. Their problems are still the control of infectious diseases, the provision of uncontaminated water supplies and proper sewage, and the elevation of the general standard of living to a minimum acceptable level. In economically more fortunate countries, however, such as the United States, Great Britain, and a number of others in western Europe, the actual problems of community health are very different. To be sure, much unfinished business remains; at the same time, a whole set of new problems has appeared. The diseases of infancy, youth, and early adulthood have been reduced to such an extent that people are no longer dying of them in large numbers. As the problems of communicable disease have declined in urgency, the community health program has broadened to include, wherever feasible, other elements and situations that may adversely affect the physical and mental well-being of people in the community. The widening horizons of public health have in recent years come to include such problems as mental health and illness, prevention of accidents, as well as renewed emphasis on the control of the physical environment. With our expanding and changing industrial technology have come environmental alterations of increasing complexity. Recent years have also brought an increasing amount of discussion of the social and psychological changes accompanying our expanding urbanism.

All these trends have their reflection in the area of child health. Some of the problems are more recent than others. The effects of radiation on child health whether through diagnostic radiology or fall-out are still largely unknown and remain to be elucidated. Similarly, the long range genetic effects of radiation are still in dispute.

On the other hand, while specific aspects of the mental health of children have indirectly received attention for well over a century, it is only recently that direct attention has been given to these matters from a more scientific viewpoint. For the most part, the earliest knowledge on the mental health of children came from persons with the responsibility of providing care for neglected, dependent, and delinquent children. During the last two decades of the nineteenth century social workers were particularly active in trying to find ways of dealing with the problem of "child saving." Behavior problems of children received attention, the importance of the home and good mothering were stressed, and on an empirical basis welfare workers developed points of view which in more recent years have either been rediscovered or reinforced in terms of dynamic theories of behavior and personality development.

Initially, the emphasis was on rehabilitation and therapy. As the value of preventing abnormal child development became increasingly apparent, efforts were directed at assisting parents in helping their children during the formative years of infancy and childhood. Nursery schools, kindergartens, parent education all played a part in helping children toward healthy physical and mental development.

To be sure, much remains to be done in the field of child health. The world in which our children live is in many ways better than it was in 1890 or 1900. Our retrospective glance showed clearly how far we have come, but it is just as clear that we cannot be satisfied with the present. The Mid-Century White House Conference on Children and Youth of 1950 took as its theme the total well-being of children or "how we can develop in children the mental, emotional, and spiritual qualities essential to individual happiness and responsible citizenship and what physical, economic, and social conditions are deemed necessary to this development." This is still the problem for the years ahead.

To achieve this purpose more effort must be focused on unsolved health problems. Most prominent among these are perinatal mortality and certain handicapping conditions, chiefly convulsive disorders, cerebral palsy, and mental retardation which appear to be associated with conditions and circumstances affecting fetal development and birth. In this connection the significance of nutrition requires further intensive investigation. The accumulation and application of new knowledge about premature births would probably make it possible not only to reduce neonatal mortality considerably, but also to prevent a large amount of later physical and mental disability.

More needs to be accomplished also in the prevention of human malformations. Except for the cases of rubella infection and of radiation, little has yet been done to translate existing knowledge of the factors involved in the experimental production of congenital malformations in animals into tools that may be useful for human populations. Similarly, there are large areas in the field of mental health that remain to be tilled. For example, the hypothesis of maternal deprivation and its effects requires more critical investigation.

Various social services to families also require expansion if we expect children to develop and grow up in a wholesome environment. The broadening concept of how home-makers can be used is an instance in point. Still another is the development of methods for prepaying and providing medical care so that continuity and quality of needed medical services may be maintained.

These are only a few indications pointing to fruitful areas of action in the next decade. Research will undoubtedly be carried on, and new knowledge relating to health and disease in children will undoubtedly accumulate. Equally important, however, is to see that such knowledge is applied for the benefit of those who need it. Social inventiveness and innovation must go hand in hand with scientific investigation if the world of the 1960s is to be a healthier one for children.

GROWING UP
IN AN AFFLUENT SOCIETY

by MOSES ABRAMOVITZ

RELIGION apart, no aspect of human affairs has such pervasive and penetrating consequences as does the way a society makes its living—and how large a living it makes. And few societies have experienced such radical alteration in the level of their income and in the manner in which it is earned as has this country during the last seventy-five years. In this period, in common with most of the countries which share in the civilization of the Western world, America has been passing through the complex series of changes we associate, however vaguely, with industrialization. Wherever this process has held sway, the application of science to industry and the accumulation of capital have transformed the economic life of peoples. But in America, these forces have operated in a peculiarly favorable environment and the transformation in the modes of living and working have been especially profound.

Industrialization has reshaped our lives, not only during

Moses Abramovitz is Research Associate of the National Bureau of Economic Research and Professor of Economics at Stanford University.

the years people work, but during those in which they are not yet old enough to work and during those in which they are too old. In this essay, however, I will try to write about the impact of industrialization, not on the whole of our mortal span, but rather on those peculiarly malleable, impressionable, and seminal years of youth—not "from the cradle to the grave," but from the cradle to the job. I will try to say something about the economic developments which have been transforming the position and prospects of American youth. And I will try also to say what I can about the significance of these changes, although this is far from clear. Indeed to descry this significance is a major challenge to study and insight so that we may, so far as we can, put ourselves in a position to understand our fate and, in some degree, to shape it.

The Rise in Income and the Change in its Distribution

The most obvious effect of industrialization upon the young has come through the change it has wrought in the incomes of the families in which they grow up. In terms of the dollar's purchasing power in 1957, the average income of American families in 1870 was roughly $1,750. This date does not represent the beginning of industrialization in this country, but it is the earliest date for which fairly reliable figures are available and it carries us back ninety years to a time when nearly three-quarters of our population was still classified as rural and when some 53 percent of those gainfully employed were still engaged in agricultural pursuits. By 1958, however, the level of living had risen beyond recognition. Average family income had increased about three and one-half times and stood at well over $6,000 per family. And since the size of families has declined—from slightly over 5 persons per family in 1870 to about 3.5 in recent years—family income today is devoted to the support of fewer children. Income per capita, in other words, has increased still faster than family income. During 1958 disposable income per head of the population stood at about $1,800, a figure five times as large as per capita disposable income in 1869 when measured in dollars with today's purchasing power.

The effects of this great rise in income upon the growth of the country ramify in many directions. Our children, like their parents, are far better fed, clothed, and housed than they used to be. This more generous provision for the physical necessities of life is reflected in their health and in that of their parents. It is well-known that the great increase in life expectancy at birth, which has risen some 50 percent since 1870, manifests itself most strikingly in the proportion of all children born who survive the dangers of infancy and childhood and live to enter adult careers. It is less well-known that the lesser, but still significant, improvement in the life expectancy of adults has significantly reduced the proportion of our children who must grow up in broken families. As late as 1900, approximately 1 out of 4 widows was under forty-five years of age. In 1956, the corresponding figure was 1 in 12.

No doubt the advance of medical science and of the scientific basis of public health has been a necessary condition for the improvement recorded in the health of children and of the population at large. But just as clearly, the rise of income has been required to provide the resources needed to support scientific work, to exploit its findings, and to spread its benefits to the mass of the population. Some portion of responsibility for the improvement of health is to be ascribed to the mere fact that a much larger portion of the population now enjoys the varied diet and the more sanitary living conditions which only the rich could afford a century ago. Some portion too must be assigned to the resources which richer communities can provide for safeguards against the contamination of water and food, against the spread of epidemics, for the sanitary disposal of waste, and for the extension of hospital and other medical facilities to every section of the population. Nor should we forget that, in contrast to conditions one hundred or even fifty years ago, very few children now grow up in families in which medical care, more especially hospital care, is denied them because of mere geographical isolation. Industrialization has implied urbanization and has bound even the most remote places to centers of population and of medical facilities with an efficient system of transport and communication.

The rise of income then has enlarged the potential of youth in the fundamental physical sense that it has contributed to a great increase in the proportion of infants born who survive throughout the entire span of childhood and adolescence and live to become adults. In short, one of the most important things about living in an affluent society is that children stand a better chance of growing up, at least in the minimal sense of reaching adulthood. The rise in income, however, has helped to enlarge the scope of youth in another, equally important, respect. Childhood and youth are vivid, active years of life, important in themselves; but they are also years of preparation for adult careers. Indeed, one of the more significant ways in which the period of youth may be defined is by the age at which a young person makes the transition from preparation for work to work itself and, by obtaining gainful employment, secures the prerequisite for a life no longer in dependence upon his parents.

In this sense too, industrialization has extended the period of youth for the mass of young people. It has done so in two ways: by placing a greater premium upon formal education as a qualification for successful participation in a career of work, and by providing the means by which a longer period of education could be extended to a larger portion of our youth.

The level of a country's income supports, or restricts, its educational system in two ways. It provides the resources from which the staffs of its schools and their physical facilities are supported, and it affords that necessary surplus of income which makes it possible to dispense with the contribution of children to the family budget. In this country, partly because the level of income was relatively high, provision for public education developed earlier than in many countries of Western Europe. Yet in 1900, while 96 percent of American children between six and fourteen were attending school, the percentage of those between fourteen and seventeen was only 15, while those attending colleges and universities were 4 percent of the population aged nineteen to twenty-two.

Thus in 1900, we were well on the way to universal elementary education, but this was as yet hardly true of secondary education, while a college education was still restricted to a very few. Today, as we know, these figures are very different. The percentage of children between six and fourteen attending school in 1957 was 99; that for the youngsters of high school age was 89; and in addition, no fewer than 20 percent of those between eighteen and twenty-four were in school, the bulk attending some institution of higher learning. We have, therefore, reached a period when secondary education, while by no means universal, is the norm, and when college or university training has been put within reach of a very large and growing minority of young people.

In so far, then, as we look on youth as a period of dependency and of preparation, the rise in income has brought us the means and, also the need, to extend the period of youth for the mass of the population. Both these aspects of the enlarged scope of youth call for our closest consideration. We have extended the years of dependency and postponed the age when young people, by earning their own living, assume a role of responsibility as well as of independence of their parents' guidance and control. But this portentous change is qualified by another which we have already noted. If the average period of dependency has been extended, so has the life expectancy of young people at the age at which they pass into the work force. The latter may not completely offset the former in the sense of keeping the proportion between years of preparation and years of activity constant, but there has been a substantial offset.

The other aspect of the enlargement of youth through education is perhaps more nearly obvious but not less fundamental. The extension of schooling means, on the whole, better formal training and, therefore, a larger range of ultimate opportunities for the much larger portion of our youth who share in them. As we shall see, however, the larger provision of education has been accompanied by a larger need, and, therefore, has aggravated the disabilities imposed on the substantial fractions of our youth who may be deprived of a chance to gain all the formal training from which they are able to benefit.

The great rise in average income during the last century has been accompanied during much of the period by a trend towards greater equality in the distribution of income. In the last thirty years, the money incomes of the relatively poor families have increased considerably more rapidly than those of the relatively rich. This was not clearly true of money incomes in earlier decades, but there is good reason to think that it was, nevertheless, true of real income. For the goods and services whose supply is especially cheapened by the introduction and improvement of power machinery and mass production are typically the kinds of goods consumed by the lower income groups. And to this we must add the considerable contribution of state services, chiefly in aid of the lower income groups, which has grown apace with the burgeoning role of government.

The more equal distribution of income is working together with the extension of education and with the change in conditions of work to make the conditions of adolescence and the prospects of youth of all classes more similar to one another than they have ever been before. The extension of education fits a larger proportion of youth for work of a type requiring formal training and makes this central experience of youth more nearly the same for large sectors of the population. At the same time, the reduction in the inequalities among their families' incomes makes their lives at home less different and brings them together in neighborhoods less divided in external appearance and in the character of the activities they harbor. The net result is presumably that youths share a more nearly similar outlook and a more nearly similar set of aspirations. It goes without saying that, in this country, the outlook and aspirations which are coming to be more widely shared are those of the middle class—but what this ever-growing, long-dominant sector of American society is becoming, thinking and aspiring to are matters I must leave to other writers.

The Changing Character of Work

The rise in income about which we have spoken is the most obtrusive aspect of industrialization and certainly the one in which we can take the most unalloyed satisfaction. But industrialization involves many great changes in the mode of economic activity and in nothing so much as in the nature of the daily jobs we do.

The most general way to characterize this change is to say that it involves a shift from the relatively direct manipulation and fabrication of things to jobs concerned with the organization and regulation of production and distribution, from hard-handed to soft-handed work, from blue-shirt to white-collar occupations. We may see this first in the great decline of farming which in 1870 still engaged some 53 percent of those gainfully employed but in 1957 employed under 10 percent of our labor force. We see it next in the lesser relative decline of the other great "commodity-producing" industries—manufacturing, mining, and construction, and in the relative growth of those departments of the economy concerned with the organization and regulation of production and the distribution of its products—that is, the services, trade, finance, the professions, and government itself. Finally, we may see it in the great increase of clerical, administrative, and overhead activity within *all* branches of economic activity. For it is in the nature of the process of industrialization and the basis of its efficiency that productive activity becomes more specialized and that machines take on more of the physical work, while men become increasingly concerned with the supervision of machines, with the coordination of specialized productive activity and the routing of its product.

Two aspects of this change are especially noteworthy in their impact on the position and prospects of youth, and both fit in with and support the forces set in motion by the income changes already described. In the first place, the change in the nature of work from unskilled to skilled occupations, from blue-shirt to white-collar, from manual manipulation to distribution, administration and regulation involves a vast increase in our need for educated people and, therefore, in the opportunities our economy affords to the educated. With regard to the kind of education that is needed, it is clear that a highly industrialized and rich society needs people with education at every level, starting with mere literacy and going on to specialized and profound training of every kind and degree. It cannot prosper without it. The process, therefore, which has given us the resources to support a longer period of preparation for an ever larger portion of our youth, has also greatly increased our need for that kind of preparation, and one of the central social questions of our time is whether we have so used our resources as to make provision for education to match our need. Nor should we forget that if one side of the coin of industrialization is the greater opportunity which is afforded to skill and education, the reverse is the barrier it sets up against the employment and advancement of young people who are deprived of formal training. Individual development, no less than social, demands that adequate provision be made for the education of every young person who can use it and that each such person be put in a position to avail himself of the facilities provided.

The change in the character of work is also acting to soften the class divisions of our society. For in this country, the chief social boundary has been the line dividing the manual, or, if one likes, proletarian occupations, from the nonmanual. Those engaged in the latter, however important the differences due to income, are broadly associated with the business, or middle, class in our society and, in a general way, share a common set of attitudes and aspirations and identify themselves with one another. Since the most prominent change in the character of work has been to effect a vast enlargement in the proportion of our population engaged in nonmanual occupations, we may assume that a larger proportion of families now identify themselves with the middle class. And, therefore, on this account, as well as on account of the extension of education and the more equal distribution of income, their children are growing up under more nearly similar circumstances and coming to share the outlook and ambitions of the middle class to which their parents see themselves as belonging.

We may well believe that such a change in the class divisions of our society has effects of the most far-reaching character upon the position of the young, their prospects, and their aims. It is far less easy to guess what these effects are and to evaluate them. We may well speculate upon the increase in social mobility when many more young people feel themselves to be members of the same dominant class, and upon the ease with which they will see themselves as moving to occupations, regions, and social strata still strange to their parents. And we may think too about what this widespread identification portends for the stability of our economic and political system. But if these vague directions of speculation give rise to any feelings of satisfaction or complacency, we should think also about what the change signifies for the variety of life in our country. And we should, in particular, consider what it means for the division between those growing up with an outlook proper to what Thorstein Veblen called "industry," as distinct from "business."

Few aspects of living shape our values and our interests more powerfully than does the concrete nature of our work-a-day lives. *Industry* is the fabrication of goods. It provides an education in the relations between physical causes and effects. Those who are concerned with it learn the properties and possibilities of materials and tools. They take from it a matter-of-fact concern with the direct and unadorned adaptation of goods to their functions, and they are led to conceive the functions of goods in their relations to the more solid needs and wants of human beings. *Business* is the making of money. As a social institution, it is the basis of the complex mechanism by which our labor and capital are guided towards the production of the goods people demand—as these demands register in markets. To those engaged in business, however, it is only in part an education in the adaptation of goods to people's needs and in the design and operation of efficient productive organizations. It is also an education in the manipulation of our needs and in the restriction of output, in the arts of bargain and maneuver, of speculation and promotion. It is an experience in the strategies by which advancement is gained in large corporations and in the tactics by which income and wealth are preserved in the face of the vagaries of markets and the exactions of governments. As the characters of children are formed in their homes rather more than in their schools, we must be deeply concerned with the impact of the changing nature of work on the everyday concerns of their parents.

The New Security in Business and Professional Careers

In view of the growth of the middle class, as distinct from the manual worker, or proletarian, class, it is worth considering some of the important ways in which the differing eco-

nomic and career outlooks of these classes are reflected in
the patterns of life of the youths who belong to them. For,
it turns out, the career outlooks of these classes have changed
along with the change in their relative size.

One of the chief differences between proletarian and middle-class life used to be that a proletarian youth left school
and got a job relatively early, and fairly soon thereafter
achieved a secure status relative to the standards of his
class. By contrast, a youth entering a middle-class occupation,
unless he was very rich, took much longer to obtain a secure
foothold. If he were going into business, he needed years in
which to accumulate the capital with which to start the
independent venture which was the normal form of business
activity, and even if he were fortunate enough to have access
to a small capital, a considerable period was needed to obtain the experience with which to use capital effectively.
Similarly, if he were entering a profession, he not only faced
many years of preparation but also an indefinite period of
insecurity thereafter while he built up at least a modest
private practice. As a result of this difference in the time-
patterns of their careers, working-class youths courted and
married relatively early, and they had more children and
had them earlier than did youths going into business and
the professions. In this respect, the working-class youth re-
sembled the young people of very rich families—though for
very different reasons.

This important point of differentiation between the life
patterns of the different classes, however, has now changed
both in its incidence and its character in the further course

of economic development. On the one hand, a larger proportion of young men, as already noted, are destined for occupations associated with the middle class and, therefore, adopt middle-class standards with regard to the time and character of courtship and marriage and with regard to the number and spacing of their children. On the other hand, it is now possible to obtain a foothold in the more characteristic middle-class occupations earlier and more easily than used to be true. Business is now generally organized in the form of large corporations rather than in small independent ventures. Young businessmen, therefore, enter their careers at the lower levels of large firms and advance through their managerial bureaucracies. Capital is not required for entrance, and experience is gained on the job.

The prospects for young professional and semi-professional aspirants have similarly improved. For one thing, the demand for people with such training has, in recent years, far outrun the growth of supply. Independent practice is, therefore, more easily established. For another, the growth in the size of business firms, in the scope and variety of governmental activities, in the importance and size of labor unions, and of medical, scientific and educational institutions, has created a host of professional and semi-professional posts within the staffs of these organizations. At the same time, what amounts to the corporate practice of professions has grown in importance. Thus, the problem of establishing an independent practice may now be by-passed by a large fraction of those entering the learned middle-class pursuits. On all these counts, the aspiring young businessman or professional may now look forward with unprecedented confidence to a secure career upon the completion of his training. Finally, although the period of training is now somewhat longer in several of the major professions than was the case a generation or two ago, it is now probably easier for a young man to obtain the means to support himself during his training. For this there are a number of reasons. The rise of incomes has made it easier for parents to provide liberal support for their children. At the same time, philanthropic and governmental support of education has provided more scholarship aid than used to be the case. Finally, students themselves, profiting by the rise of earning power, find it easier to supplement their funds by work. And when, as is not uncommon, they marry in the course of schooling, their wives can contribute to their support by exploiting new opportunities for women in industry.

The net outcome of this complex of supporting changes has been to place the future of men entering middle-class occupations upon a secure basis at a much earlier age than was true even a generation ago. As a consequence early courtship, marriage, and family foundation are now more feasible for this group. In this respect, as in others already noted, the attitudes and life patterns of middle-class youth have come to resemble those of the working class and of the very rich. It would, of course, be imprudent to assert that the relatively new patterns of high-school courtships, much earlier marriage, of larger numbers of children more closely spaced, which has become characteristic of middle-class youth, as well as of the young of other classes, can be accounted for entirely, or even chiefly, by the economic developments traced above. Whatever the contributing circumstances, however, we can be confident that so large a change in the life patterns of middle-class youth could not have taken place except upon a firm economic basis.

The New Position of Women

Because men have been, and still are, more closely concerned with economic activity than women, much of the discussion so far has been concerned more with the position and prospects of boys and young men, rather than with those of girls and young women. In the more recent development of our economy, however, the working life of women, with some inevitable differences, has come to resemble that of men more closely than ever before. This, in turn, has affected the prospects of women, it has had a significant impact on their activities as youths, and raised certain problems concerning their schooling and the course of their early careers.

In industrialized societies, it has long been normal for men, except for farmers, to work outside the home. Until recently, however, the great bulk of women in America have spent the major portion of their adult lives inside the home. It is true that it was common for unmarried girls to seek outside employment during the period between the end of their schooling and their marriage. And it is also true that widows, as well as married women in the lowest income groups, were forced to seek employment to help support themselves and their families. By and large, however, the great bulk of married women occupied themselves with household duties. In 1890, women made up only some 16 percent of those gainfully employed, and married women were only 14 percent of the total number of women at work. By 1958, however, women constituted 32 percent of the labor force and over 50 percent of the women at work were married. The role of work in the lives of women has, therefore, changed considerably. In former decades, girls worked, if at all between end of school and marriage, and then confined themselves, as a rule, to household occupations. In recent years, however, they tend to remain in school longer and marry earlier, which restricts the frequency and length of premarital employment. On the other hand, as already noted, they have their children earlier, and they then enter the labor market in very large numbers as soon as the youngest of their children reach school age. And since the life-span of women is now longer than it used to be, many married women experience a long period of work outside the home.

This considerable transformation in the working life of women reflects the combined impact of a number of economic causes directly and indirectly. In the first place, there is the change in the character of work from manual labor to office work of various kinds, which has created a large number of jobs deemed suitable for women in our society. In addition, the early foundation and completion of families leaves women with reduced household duties at a time of life when they are still active and vigorous. Next, the wider spread of middle-class standards of living imposes on women the need to help their families sustain such standards both in ordinary consumption and in the education of their children. It is, perhaps, not too much to say that in former decades children left school early to make money to help support their parents at working-class standards. More recently, however, mothers feel impelled to leave their homes to make money to help provide consumption goods and schooling for their children at middle-class standards. We must add finally that the entrance of women, especially married women, into work has been substantially eased by the fact that hours of work are now shorter, leaving them a larger amount of time to devote to children and household duties than was previously available to a working woman, and that homes are now easier to manage, thanks to the improvements in household equipment and the transfer of many household tasks to the commercial economy.

The fact that many women now feel impelled to enter gainful employment for a substantial portion of their married lives and that opportunities to do so now exist has already had some effect on the upbringing and education of girls and presumably should have still more. We note, first, that the great bulk of girls now attend and finish high school and that a considerable fraction of them continue their education in college and beyond. Not only is secondary and higher education for young women more widespread, it is now conducted with an eye somewhat more intent on the occupational and professional implications of such education. It is by no means clear, however, that the process of modifying the upbringing and education of girls has as yet gone as far as it might in view of the working life which is now in prospect for a considerable fraction of women. At least two areas of possible action need to be studied. First, curricula for

women both in high school and college which used to have
dominantly nonoccupational aims need to be reconsidered
to achieve a proper balance between the contribution they
can make to the work careers of women and to the other
objectives of education. Secondly, young girls and women
need to be made more aware than they already are about
the career choices now open to them, about the kinds of
training they can obtain, and about the way in which premarital work experience can help fit them for the much
longer period of work many of them will desire after their
children have entered school.

The New Standards of Consumption and Leisure

We have so far been concerned chiefly with the economic
development of the country upon the lives of our youth as
this has acted through the changes in work patterns and in
preparation for work. But the great rise in income, of course,
has accomplished a change not only in the working lives of
the bulk of our families, but also in their lives outside of
work. Two aspects of this change seem especially noteworthy.
In the first place, the great majority of families now enjoy
an income which provides a substantial surplus with which
they can buy goods and services yielding pleasure, as contrasted with commodities required to meet the necessities of
nourishment, clothing, and shelter. In the second place, we
have chosen to transform our enormous rise in productivity
only partly into higher incomes. In good part, we have chosen
to substitute fewer hours of work and more hours of leisure
for the still higher incomes we might otherwise have. Thus,

in 1890, a representative worker in a nonagricultural job would have worked an average of some fifty-eight hours per week. Today, he works only some thirty-nine hours per week, a change which has approximately doubled the effective leisure time at the disposal of employed persons. By contrast with the situation two or three generations ago, adults now have more goods to enjoy and more leisure time in which to enjoy them. Pleasure, play, community affairs, and non-work activities in general, it may be said, have now become, perhaps for the first time, substantial parts of the daily lives of the ordinary run of men and women.

The full implications of this striking, almost revolutionary change in the character of ordinary life are still far from clear. Two aspects of the matter, however, are quite closely tied to the themes already sounded. One is that fathers, like mothers, can now be with their families for a considerable portion of each day and week. The result has been a quickening and intensification of family life, and the family is again the center of youth's activities to a degree not experienced in urban communities for several generations. The return of the father to the family, however, has been in a rather new role —not as breadwinner, but as participant in the leisure-time activities of the family. One may categorize the change, somewhat too strongly perhaps, by saying that it was characteristic of an earlier and poorer generation that a major concern of family life was the effort of fathers to stimulate and govern the early stages of their sons' work activities. It is characteristic of our own more abundantly provided generation that a major concern of family life is the effort by sons—and daughters—to stimulate and govern the leisure-time activities of their fathers. However this may be, there is little doubt that fathers now share much more fully in the daily lives of their families and that family activities are now more largely concerned with things other than work than ever before. It may well be worth thinking whether this change in the pattern of family life is not connected in a significant way with the recent trend toward early courtship and marriage and with the tendency of young couples to have larger families earlier in their married life.

The new patterns of consumption and leisure may also be playing an important part in forming the goals and ambitions of youth as they look toward their careers in business. A long series of students from de Tocqueville in the 1820s to Andre Seigfried in the 1920s concurred in the finding that an intense and wholehearted dedication to the life of business and the goal of making (more) money was a distinctive characteristic of the American middle class. More recently, however, a new shade has been detected in the outlook of middle-class youth. Determined as ever to win a place in the world of work and to invest a major effort in this sphere, their dedication to the notion that their own goal, like America's, is success in business is no longer unqualified. They still look forward to careers that will win for them a secure status at a level perhap better in most cases than their parents enjoyed. But more frequently, they seek to do so in jobs that will not demand from them the same intense application that their fathers and grandfathers were willing, and even eager, to accept. They are concerned, rather, to achieve a more even balance between the portion of their lives devoted to business or professional work and that which they are free to devote to their families, to the leisure-time activities in which their wives and children share, and to the affairs of the communities in which they live. We are challenged to consider how this more balanced, but less intensely pursued, round of activities will alter the quality of the satisfactions yielded by their lives. And we must also think how this more qualified devotion of our energies to business may influence the further economic development of the country.

"The child is the father of the man." For better or worse, the attitudes towards work, leisure, and consumption which will give tone to American civilization during the next generations are now being formed in our children. Their values and aspirations are emerging from the experience they now share with their parents and peers as we all learn to enjoy—to use or dissipate—our still new-won prosperity. Our own lives, private and public, will tell whether the affluence we now enjoy and the still more abounding productive powers which our children will control will be worthily used or most thoughtlessly squandered.

THE IMPACT OF URBANIZATION

by JEAN GOTTMANN

URBANIZATION today is a powerful trend, deeply modifying both the environmental conditions and the inner structure of modern society. Its impact on the majority of the people in Western countries cannot be too carefully studied. It is a particularly strong force in the United States because of the tremendous number of people involved.

The younger generation, most of whom today are born and grow up away from the farm, feels this impact in two ways: first, the environment of their childhood and adolescence is urban; second, the system to which they will eventually have to adapt their adult life is urban. This is no longer simply a steady flow from the farms to the towns. Urbanization today is one of the more striking expressions of the sweeping and profound changes now developing in the organization of society, and American-style urban growth is being reproduced increasingly in many other lands. Its impact carries the need for reassessing many of the values held and the

Jean Gottmann is Research Director, Study of Megalopolis, Twentieth Century Fund, and Professor, Ecole des Hautes Etudes, University of Paris.

measures adopted for the welfare and education of children
and youth.

Momentum and New Forms of Urbanization

Urban growth is no more a phenomenon affecting only a
small fraction of the total population and several isolated
spots over a vast country. In the United States the population in urban territory rose from 45.7 percent of the total in
1910 to 64 percent in 1950. The farm population meanwhile
declined to 15.3 percent in 1950 and probably to 11.7 percent
by April, 1956. Farming is now the occupation of less than
1 out of 10 Americans; more than 90 percent of the nation
live from and by activities of an urban type. Similar percent-
ages are being achieved or forecast for many countries in
Western Europe advanced in industrialization. The trend is
worldwide and appears irreversible: the progress of agricultural techniques and farm mechanization make it possible
to produce more agricultural goods with less and less hands.
Thus a migration from farm to city goes on and must be
accelerated as large numbers come of age in farming areas.

For years the terms urban and rural have represented the
major dichotomy in the division of human labor and in the
classification of landscapes. On one hand the green countryside was the locale of agricultural production. On the other
hand the built-up, crowded, urbanized areas were the sites
of manufacturing, trade, government, worship, and recreation. The rural territory extended over almost the whole land
and rural life was reputed simple, natural, and healthy. Cities
occupied small parcels of land surrounded with walls or bou-

levards, isolated spots amid rural territory, and were usually criticized as offering an artificial, unhealthy, complicated way of life. These old contrasts still exist in underdeveloped parts of the world. They are a tale of bygone days in the more advanced countries and especially in the United States.

Since more than 90 percent of the population now live by pursuits other than farming, i.e., by activities within the categories of industry, trade, services, and government, usually located in cities, urban territory cannot be expected to remain limited to a few small spots on the map. Urbanization has taken on a size and a momentum that has reversed old concepts of simple contrasts between urban and rural. Cities have broken out of old bounds and scattered buildings of urban aspect and functions all over the countryside, thus coming to occupy vast regions. The U.S. Census has had a hard time trying to keep up with these trends. As suburbs mushroomed around the old urban centers defined as *cities,* the Census established first the notion of *urbanized areas,* which consisted mainly of densely built-up territory. Then, in 1940, there was introduced the *metropolitan area,* a wider concept encompassing entire counties whose economy appears tightly dependent on a central city.[1] By 1950 the area of many of these standard metropolitan areas had to be extended and the population of the 174 areas in the continental United States totalled 85.5 million or 57 percent of the nation. In 1950 the majority of Americans lived in metropolitan regions; this does not mean they all lived in densely built-up

[1] See definitions and statistical data in *County and City Data Book* 1956 (Washington, D.C.: U.S. Bureau of the Census, 1957).

districts, for a metropolitan area may well include green, rural looking sections, but its inhabitants engage in little agricultural activity and are primarily dependent for their livelihood on the connection with a central city of more than 50,000 people.

From 1940 to 1950, while the total population of the United States increased by 14.5 percent, the population of metropolitan areas grew by 22.2 percent. Since 1950 this latter rate of growth has accelerated. The Bureau of the Census estimated the growth of the country's civilian population between 1950 and 1956 to be 9.8 percent and that of the metropolitan areas to be 14.8 percent; but in many cases the peripheral growth has spilled over these limits into territory classified as non-metropolitan in 1950. There is no doubt that the 1960 Census will have to add many new counties to the list of those classified as metropolitan and it will then be recognized that the rate of increase of metropolitan population is more than 50 percent faster than the nation's growth. Thus we see that modern urbanization takes on original forms which scatter the urban functions and population around the countryside. While the old migration from farms towards towns goes on, the towns spread out in irregular fashion back into the formerly rural countryside.

For some time now the Census has distinguished between rural farm and rural nonfarm population. In any agricultural region some nonfarm activities are needed to service the farms. In an area of large and highly mechanized farms the nonfarm population may become more numerous than the farm population which it services; in such cases however a good part of it will be concentrated in towns of some size, and counted as urban rather than rural nonfarm. In any case it seems obvious that when the rural nonfarm element of a rural territory of a small region reaches a large majority, and in some cases it goes over 75 percent, the region depends on means of sustenance other than local agriculture.

A map of the United States showing the proportion of rural nonfarm population in rural territory by county demonstrates such a process of gradual de-ruralization over vast stretches. The map (fig. 1), giving the situation in 1950, well illustrates one stage of a trend which has progressed since then and will undoubtedly continue in the next decades. Farming will hardly need more lands; an increased consumption of farm products may be satisfied by reducing the surpluses and increasing, if need be, the yields over much of the major agricultural regions. The "de-ruralization" ought to gain in the Northeast (where it was already quite advanced in 1950), in the Southeast, some parts of the West, and even of the Midwest.

Modern urbanization has invaded so widely the regions formerly held as rural but without densely building them up, that the distinction between urban and rural in the old sense calls for revision. Unofficial proposals have suggested new terms such as "outer-suburbia," "exurbia," "interurbia," and recently sociologists offered to call these scattered populations "rurban." All such terms include some hint at the urban nature of the new areas and as they develop beside officially urban territory we may well speak of a degree of suburbanization (as fig. 1 indicates) pending new official definitions.

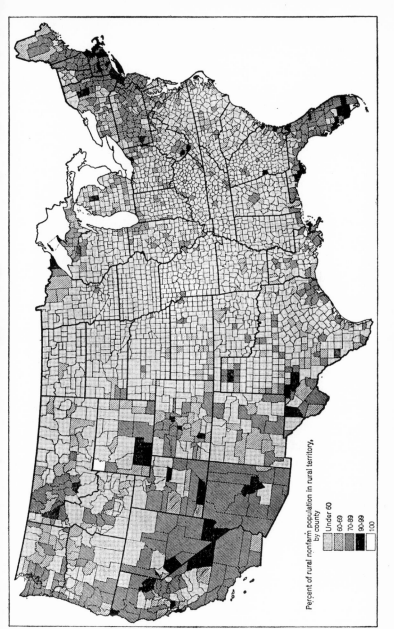

Percent of rural nonfarm population in rural territory,
by county

Under 60
60-69
70-89
90-99
100

Figure 1. Suburbanization in the United States, 1950
Courtesy of the Twentieth Century Fund

Urbanization has taken on a new, nebulous kind of structure.[2] This results from the scattering of residences as well
as from the centering of large shopping centers or important
manufacturing plants at rural crossroads and in small towns.[3]
It is also due to the development of rural regions, some of
which were until recently being depopulated, for recreational
activities in the mountains or at the seashore. Altogether this
process of urbanization causes new forms of land use and a
new system of relations within a community, between communities, and between individuals and their environment.

The Revolution in Land Use

It would be far too simple to sum up the major effects of
modern urbanization by stressing the sprawl of suburban
or metropolitan patterns over vast areas against farming's
retreat to more limited, specialized regions. The two trends
coexist but do not conflict on a large scale. True, in some
suburban areas such as central Long Island and much of
New Jersey, new developments have crowded out many farms
in recent years. But on the whole and for many years the
abandonment of tilled land has proceeded faster than the
occupation of land for urban and interurban uses. This was
still true on the whole throughout the United States even in
the 1950s although land has been devoured for urban use at
an estimated pace of a million acres per year. Total cropland

[2] See Otis Dudley Duncan and Albert J. Reiss, Jr., *Social Characteristics of Urban and Rural Communities, 1950* (New York: Wiley,
1956), especially part II, pp. 117–79.
[3] The latter pattern is spreading especially in the Southeast; see for
instance Jean Gottmann, *Virginia at Mid-Century* (New York: Holt,
1955), chapter 7.

shrank from 1950 to 1954 by 10 million acres and total pasture and grazing area by 20 million acres. Woodland and forest land not used for grazing increased in the same four years by 28 million acres. The result of the present urbanization of the American population and economy is that the land is becoming greener and the country is reverting to a more natural condition.[4]

Whoever has recently traveled through or flown over the forested East has seen patches of land reoccupied by brush and young woods all over the countryside. In New England the increase of the wooded area since the beginning of the century and even in the last ten years has been substantial. This has happened not only in Maine and Vermont but also in the "suburbanized" states of Massachusetts, Rhode Island, and Connecticut. Similar trends can be observed over much of New York, Pennsylvania, Maryland and Virginia. It is interesting that woods are still increasing in and around the highly metropolitanized section on the northeastern seaboard which we call *Megalopolis* (from southern New Hampshire to northern Virginia, see fig. 2). This most impressive and continued chain of metropolitan regions contains one-fifth of the population of the United States on less than 2 percent of its land area.

Thus, even in the vicinity of the most crowded region in America, there still are more green spaces, and curiously enough more wildlife, than some fifty to sixty years ago.

[4] The above figures are based on the *Statistical Abstract of the United States 1958* (Washington, D.C.: U.S. Bureau of the Census, 1958), Table No. 791, p. 612. See also on what follows Jean Gottmann, "The Revolution in Land Use," in *Landscape*, Santa Fe, New Mexico, Vol. 8, No. 2 (Winter, 1959), pp. 15–21.

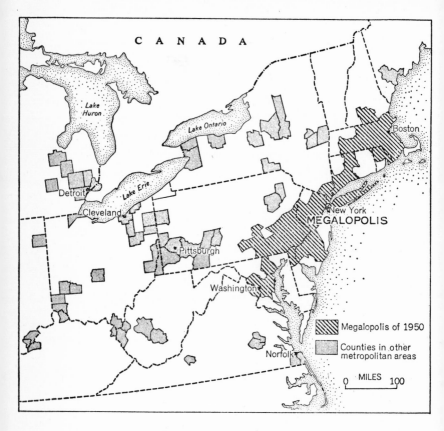

Figure 2. Megalopolis

Megalopolis is the continuous chain of counties of metropolitan economy as defined for 1950 by the U. S. Bureau of the Census (in *State Economic Areas*). It stretches from southern New Hampshire to northern Virginia, the greatest such area in the United States, encompassing about one-fifth of the total population.

Courtesy of the Twentieth Century Fund

These areas have great potential for educational and recreational opportunity. Of course such areas, almost suburban by their location, are not turning wild. The woods and brush are divided up by major highways along which ribbons of suburbs develop, while residences scatter along "rural" roads. In certain areas such residences may be occupied only for a season in the year, but increasingly they are year-round homes. In these same areas some agricultural production, yielding high profits, may take place. Lancaster county, Pennsylvania, for example, classified as a "standard metropolitan region," is also one of the richest counties in North America by virtue of its farm production. It has developed a most interesting interpenetration of urban and rural life; its farms specialize in the production of milk, meat, and poultry, i.e., in a processing stage of the agricultural cycle. The basic materials (grain, feed, and hay) are imported from afar. Indeed the new process of urbanization has created suburbs that look like farming areas used to look, and agricultural centers that look like suburbs because of the concentration of buildings. Certain types of farms, which are extremely well maintained, are actually in suburban territory because they are "estate" or "part-time" farms. A new way of life, properly suburban, has developed, for gentleman farmers are not, as in days of yore, gentlemen because they are big farmers, they are farmers because they are gentlemen with large enough incomes in the city to permit them to farm avocationally.

The rapid shifts in the land use do not affect only the rural-looking outer suburbs; they have at least as much impact on land use in the urbanized areas. In the old urban cores, the residential population is still increasing [5] but slowly, at a lower rate than in the nation as a whole, (4.7 percent increase in the central cities of standard metropolitan areas from 1950 to 1956, while the nation's increase was estimated at 9.8 percent); the metropolitan areas outside the central cities increased much faster (about 29.3 percent); and within the metropolitan areas the rural parts grew fastest (55.8 percent, adding 6 million people in six years!).

These figures concern places of residence. Much of the population in rural areas commutes to work in urban territory; and there is substantial commuting from city to city. Thus in the early 1950s close to 1,600,000 people residing elsewhere came to Manhattan to work; close to 450,000 went to Newark, N.J., to work, a figure slightly above the resident population of Newark as recorded by the Census. In most other large cities the numbers of commuters on weekdays reach hundreds of thousands. Despite endeavors at decentralization in the most crowded urban hubs, the numbers of people commuting to work have been on the increase through the 1940s and the 1950s. The Bureau of the Census, recognizing the inadequacy of recording population figures by place of residence, intends to introduce a new question about the place of work in the 1960 count.

Urbanization, in the modern sense, creates a growing dichotomy between daytime and nighttime populations in large cities. This is reinforced by the housing picture: as the trend of moving out to the periphery accelerates, the old urban core harbors age and decay. The houses emptied by

[5] No more in New York City where a 1957 census showed a decrease since 1950.

middle-income occupants who prefer to move out to the suburbs or further are taken over by tenants in the lower-income brackets who cannot afford to commute far and who often cannot for reasons of social discrimination find lodging in the highly suburban communities. Negroes and Puerto Ricans are so crowded into the large central cities that some among them commute to jobs in the suburbs. The colored population is increasing faster than the total resident population in Manhattan and Brooklyn, Washington, D.C., Baltimore, Chicago, and Philadelphia. The same trend is notable in smaller cities, especially in the highly urbanized northeast, such as Trenton or Hartford. All these cities have active business districts; but the kinds of people who walk the central city streets in daytime are increasingly different from those who are abroad at night. As urban renewal proceeds in such cities contrasts may sharpen for some of their central districts attract only affluent residents who can afford the higher costs. Even if they do not decay as residential areas,[6] central cities become sites of great contrasts between opposite extremes of the income scale. This is especially and spectacularly so in New York City and Washington, D.C. In Washington, the urban renewal of Georgetown sharpened the contrast. These growing differences between residents and daytime population are not conducive to social happiness and relaxation of tension.

Another set of contrasting patterns has developed between the different parts of a metropolitan region: in addition to the differences between the population by night and by day

[6] Raymond Vernon, *The Changing Economic Function of the Central City* (New York: Committee for Economic Development, 1959).

and the range of income levels, the suburbs have a different set of economic activities (besides the dormitory function) and an age and educational level substantially at variance with the central cities. The suburban population today as a whole is better educated, and has better housing and more recreational facilities within easy reach than the population in the urban core. With the exception of a few very large cities, the downtown areas of old urban cores are losing a good deal of their special functions as the center of the retail and entertainment trades. The present revolution in land-use results from many factors, among which perfected automobile transportation, the rising standard of living for the average family, and constantly increasing specialization of labor are probably the three main agents. This revolution in land-use ought to bring much improvement to American modes of living, learning, working, and relaxing. Whether the progress of urbanization can be made to serve such improvement is a major responsibility of our time.

Children and Youth in Urbanized Environment

The 1950 Census showed the suburban population to be slightly younger than the central city population. In all urbanized areas combined, the median age was 32.7 in central cities and 30.9 in the suburbs. It was observed that "the smaller the urbanized area, the greater is the difference in median age between central city and suburbs." [7] The age pyramid reveals a larger than average number of persons less

[7] Duncan and Reiss, *Social Characteristics of Urban and Rural Communities*, p. 120.

than twenty years of age in the suburbs. If similar statistics were available for the rural nonfarm population living within metropolitan areas, such differences would be even sharper. The quoted remark about the size of the "urbanized area" is significant: the larger the central city the further away extends its maximum commuting range. Many more people working in New York or Chicago can afford a residence for their families beyond the officially defined "urbanized area" than would be possible for people who work in Cincinnati or Albuquerque.

During the 1950s the migration to a metropolitan periphery of urban families with small children has probably been massive, especially from the larger cities, and the suburban areas ought to be "younger than ever" in the early 1960s. The usual reason a head of household gives for moving out is: "I am doing it for the children." It is also usual that the return from the suburbs to a central city is made by parents when the children, grown up, have left home. The same move also brings back to urban cores widows and widowers and even retired couples. From 1930 to 1950, the proportion of persons aged sixty-five and over in the nation went up from 5.5 percent to 8.1 percent; but it more than doubled in New York City. Nevertheless, the great metropolis was still below the national average, with the exception of Manhattan where it stood at 8.7 percent. Queens with 7.1 percent, the Bronx with 7.3 percent, and Brooklyn with 7.4 percent already reflected semi-suburban rates. New York City was surrounded with suburban counties where the proportion of aged people was below 8 percent, with the excep-

tion of the counties of Westchester and Rockland, N.Y.
A similar situation was observed around Philadelphia, Baltimore, and Washington, but Boston, and New England as
a whole, showed rather higher proportions of aged people.

The distribution of children less than fifteen years old in
1950 followed a somewhat different pattern in the highly
urbanized Northeastern seaboard from that in the rest of the
country. On the whole New York City had a low concentration; the proportion in the various counties of the metropolitan region varied between 17 and 24 percent, while the national average stood at 26.9 percent. Three states of southern New England showed slightly higher figures than did
New York City but the average was still below 26 percent in
all counties but one, and the same was true of rather suburbanized New Jersey and eastern Pennsylvania. The ratio of
children picked up quickly in the Pennsylvanian Appalach-
ians to the west, and south from Maryland and Virginia.
The South has always had a higher birth rate than the Northeast; urbanization is not the only major factor in the distribution of children through the United States. It remains
however quite clear on the map of Megalopolis that suburban districts have a higher ratio of children than the central
urban cores. In 1950 this was the case around Manhattan,
Boston, Philadelphia, Baltimore, and Washington. By 1960
the suburbs may well have a higher ratio than the nation as
a whole.

The distribution of the youth, i.e., of persons aged fifteen
to twenty-four in 1950 was not very different from the general
pattern of children, but one significant difference may be

noted. The old urban cores often showed higher rates than the outlying suburbs. This was true of Boston, Philadelphia, Baltimore, and New York City as a whole, though not of Manhattan alone. The presence of colleges in these cities and the greater opportunity offered to young job-seekers are probably the main reasons for the attraction of youngsters, especially in the ages between nineteen and twenty-four, towards the urban hubs.

The local variations of the age pyramid confirm that children are being born and reared in the United States largely away from the main urban centers but increasingly not very far away. These statistics result partly from the inheritance of a traditional geographic distribution little related to modern urbanization trends, but partly also from the choice of the parents to move towards the metropolitan periphery. As the youngsters grow closer to coming of age they are increasingly drawn towards the urban centers not only by their work but also for residence. Finally, as the old urban cores have ratios of old and young people below the national average, they have a higher than average ratio of the adult and mature population (i.e., in the ages of twenty-five to sixty-four). This is true even of nighttime residents; the ratio is of course much higher for the daytime population as the commuters into the urban hubs are predominantly in these age brackets. Thus, although children today spend most of their time away from the cities (in the more crowded, densely occupied and built-up sense of the term "city"), they will usually spend at least part of their lives in a highly urbanized environment.

The whole evolution of the labor force indicates the growth of typically urban employment in nonagricultural and nonindustrial types of activities, or, according to a slightly different classification, the expansion of the white-collar labor force over the blue-collar. The vast majority of today's children will spend their later lives in urban or suburban work and residence. The education of most youngsters should therefore be definitely urban-oriented; it should also be more advanced for a larger proportion of the upcoming generation, as an increasing proportion of all jobs require more training, more skill, and involve more responsibility.

The isolated farm and the tightly knit and relatively isolated community of the small town in a truly rural region produce only a small minority of the younger generation. Does the present type of urban and suburban growth benefit the younger strata of the nation? For a long time it was traditionally held that boys from the farms or agricultural areas in general were a "better quality" of men, had more basic virtues—in brief were better prepared for life than city boys. This belief was not only American. It was also generally held in Europe. This writer grew up and went to school in the very crowded and large metropolis of Paris; he was taught, until he became a graduate student, that the farm population was the main strength, the backbone of France. However, he also knew, from everything he heard, that the leadership of the country, the policy makers in every field came from the schools located in the center of Paris to which he and his neighbors went. These two concepts did not seem to him contradictory but rather complementary: the countryside supplied the good solid rank and file; the leadership, predominantly urban, became strong through its rank and file following. But it seemed better taste not to insist on the latter proposition and simply to stress the virtues of rural education in which rural populations eagerly believed.

Systematic sociological studies of the early schooling and adult behavior of farm boys and city boys have exploded the old myth of the superiority of rural origin. A scholarly analysis of the records of the U.S. Armed Forces has recently shown in convincing fashion that the recruits from farming areas were on the whole less prepared for modern life than urban recruits.[8] The advantages of an urban environment for children and youth, especially in the industrialized nations of the West, were to be expected. The better organized and more strictly controlled system of supply of the large urban consuming markets has led to better nutrition. Even today in New York City it is difficult to find children (unless recently arrived there) with serious nutritional deficiencies. Water and milk have been made safer to drink in the large cities, precisely because of the dangers of infection and contamination inherent in the crowding in urban environment. Modern police forces are made necessary by the problems of crowded metropolises; and despite the merited outcry against criminality and juvenile delinquency, it ought to be recognized that people in the great urbanized areas of today are much safer by virtue of the policing and the legislation in

[8] Eli Ginzberg et al., *The Ineffective Soldier* (New York: Columbia University Press, 1959), 3 vols. See also to the same effect the results of an analysis of civilian statistics in Eleanor H. Bernert, *America's Children* (New York: Wiley, 1958).

force than their ancestors used to be in a rural environment.

The general progress of civilization has brought about improvements in nutrition, health, and security at the same time as it brought about urbanization. There is no direct relationship between, say, urban growth on one hand and better health conditions on the other. The latter could be achieved without the former and vice versa. It has happened at times. However it has been mankind's, and particularly America's experience that in the long run the two proceeded hand in hand. Similarly such modern trends as the rise of juvenile delinquency and of nervous disorders in modern society ought not to be associated too closely, as they often are, with urban growth. The latter is, like the trends, a simultaneous product of the modern evolution of society; it does not determine them. The evil in society is of course concentrated wherever society itself is gathered. Crowding especially in its beginnings may cause the worst trends to intensify, but it also compensates this effect by working out legal and social antidotes. If it does not the people involved are at fault rather than the impersonal process. In the early nineteenth century, the first stages of the industrial revolution caused crowding of ill-paid industrial workers in slums in many cities. But social evolution has established today in American cities conditions of living and working for youngsters quite different from those denounced by Charles Dickens a century ago.

Today urban areas can confidently claim better organized health and educational services than rural areas. Charities, hospitals, welfare organizations can function better in a large community than in rural areas and the urban communities can afford these services more easily in terms of both adequate financing and competent personnel. If they are lacking, it is not because of the density of population or of the size of the community, but because of the spirit of the people. In India, as a noted sociologist observed, sacred cows flock into the large cities because they know they will find food and care more readily available there! Urbanization, properly managed, should benefit children and adolescents as well as other sections of the population needing help and care. Modern urbanization, however, with its differentiations between place of work and place of residence on one hand, between central city, suburbs, and outer suburbia on the other, requires that more thought and study be given to the new problems and opportunities it has helped to create.

Assets and Liabilities of Urban and Suburban Areas

As the central parts of cities continue to specialize in the functions traditionally concentrated in the "downtown" areas, children residing there may lose some of the advantages previously associated with cities of large size. The financial burden on the city government may become too great for it to maintain adequate services for residents who cannot offer a strong and expanding tax base. The city, having to provide adequate facilities for the noontime tide of business activities finds increasing difficulty in also meeting the welfare, health, educational, and recreation needs of a poorer resident population.

In the suburbs, meanwhile, because of the momentum of the metropolitan sprawl, local government is faced with such a rapid rise in the needs for facilities of all kinds that resources can seldom keep pace with the demand. Many suburban towns have trouble in providing adequate sewage for their rapidly expanding population. The schools are crowded and not always staffed with as qualified teaching personnel as the pupils' parents wish for.

The case of the schools is a constant issue because of the present trends of urbanization. Urban areas normally offer better schools and have a better educated population than the rural regions.

This latter proposition is true today of the suburban towns and of the daytime population of central cities rather than for the residents of old urban cores. A map of the percentage of the adult population on the Northeastern seaboard having completed high school or more in 1950 (see fig. 3) shows in clear fashion that the larger cities in Megalopolis have a lower ratio than their immediate suburbs. Otherwise the metropolitan areas show up better than the rural countryside and that contrast is especially sharp south of Washington, D.C. This map, based on the 1950 census, shows considerable progress all over this section when compared with a similar map for 1940. The 1960 census will undoubtedly testify to much higher ratios, and probably to greater contrasts between city and suburbs in the Northeast, and possibly between city and rural areas in the South.

As the many stages of production, agricultural as well as industrial, are being mechanized, employers are growing more

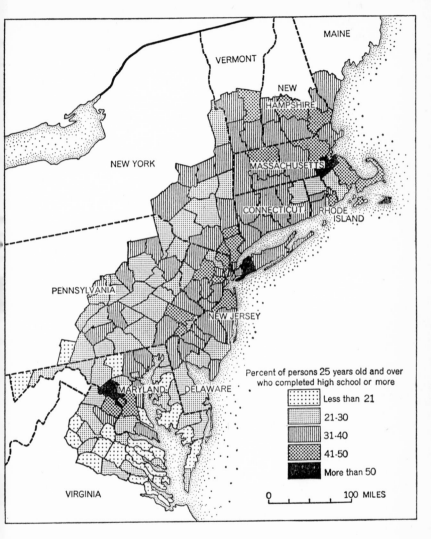

Figure 3. Education in Megalopolis, 1950
Courtesy of the Twentieth Century Fund

insistent on higher educational levels for the average employee. "Completing high school or more" will soon be a prerequisite for most occupations. Cities have attracted so many people for decades because they offered greater economic opportunity; to take advantage of it, educational achievement daily becomes more essential—and an education that can seldom be replaced by early occupational experience. To provide the younger generation with adequate educational opportunity is an imperative necessity for a nation which wants to maintain national progress and the processes of democracy. The difficulties of the central cities and of the expanding suburbs in providing adequate programs for their schools now become disturbing concerns.

In a timely report on the high schools, Dr. James B. Conant stresses the great variety of these encountered throughout the United States. He speaks for a "comprehensive high school" whose programs would correspond to "the educational needs of *all* the youth of the community." But the survey shows that there are seldom entirely comprehensive high schools and the report prefers to speak of a "degree of comprehensiveness." In some cases high schools specialize in preparing their pupils for college and higher education. "High schools whose comprehensiveness is thus limited by the nature of the community are to be found particularly in suburban areas and in high income residential sections of large cities." There are suburban high schools which may not have the same problems in supplying an adequate degree of "comprehensiveness" as the large city high school. Selective academic high schools, designed for

the academically talented youth, are found "in many of the
Eastern cities of considerable size and in a few of the medium-
sized cities." Such specialization of one or a few high schools
among many more in that city seems to favor the comprehensiveness of the system as a whole. The small high school
presents more complicated problems: "The enrollment of
many American public high schools is too small to allow a
diversified curriculum except at exorbitant expense. The
prevalence of such high schools—those with graduating
classes of less than one hundred students—constitutes one of
the serious obstacles to good secondary education throughout most of the United States." [9]

These remarks indicate that the long-range educational
consequences of urbanization will be favorable. The report
leaves aside however the question of adequate financing in
the forthcoming years, when the number of high-school
students in the medium-sized cities and the suburbs will
rapidly swell. The conclusions concerning the small high
schools make one wonder about the results of the partitioning of the mushrooming suburbs into smaller communities.
Will the less affluent suburban towns find the resources for
adequately comprehensive high schools? Moreover, this suburban partitioning may affect the children's education in other
ways and before the high-school age.

Years ago, the variety of urban life and the city's activities,
its location at a crossroads, even its crowding, offered a picture
of the world's variety and of society's problems which was

[9] James B. Conant, *The American High School Today: A First Report to Interested Citizens* (New York: McGraw-Hill, 1959), Section
IV, pp. 77–95.

stimulating and often provided the children with enriching experiences. Although it is possible to spend a long life in a metropolis without seeing anything beyond a closed local circle, urban life offers many incentives to learn how to feel the pulse of a wide, complicated, striving world. This is an important aspect of educational opportunity at a time of rapid change, of growing interregional and international exchanges and interdependence. Here is an advantage available to youngsters who fully profit from the urban environment. Some of them will of course react negatively to the challenge and early build up an attitude of blasé sophistication, hoping to thus protect themselves from the on-rushing outside world.

As one reads the many volumes recently published on suburban life, one is impressed with the frequent endeavor of the new communities to remain homogeneous, tightly organized, and somewhat isolated from the surrounding areas. Such hints can easily be gathered from works such as: A. C. Spectorsky's *The Exurbanites*, John Keats' *The Crack in the Picture Window*, William H. Whyte's *The Organization Man*, etc. Such homogeneity may help solve many local problems and avoid others characteristic of more diversified groups. It may also take away from the youngsters' education and experience many valuable assets provided by the usual urban conditions, for the sheltered environment of such suburban towns does not always prepare children for real life in the outside world. The size of the town is not significant in this respect. Such closed-in communities have existed in large cities. The multiplication of such compartments in the suburbs does not necessarily entail an isolated education as the town is within easy reach of some bustling business district and of several very different towns. The fashion for such homogeneous suburbs appears indicative however of a psychological attitude favoring social isolation which may well be going against society's present trends.

As one wishes to see today the complexities of the urbanized areas put to better use, with an aim of familiarizing youth with the variety and complexity of the world, one also wonders whether cities and suburbs take full advantage of the educational and recreational assets offered by the expanding woods in their vicinity and by the growing interpenetration of suburban residential, manufacturing, and specialized farming areas. The variety of neighborhoods within a metropolitan region is often astonishing. The proximity to existing green belts is generally greater than usually expected. The access to these green belts and to this wide gamut of economic institutions is worth many theoretical lessons to children reared in built-up residential neighborhoods. Such educational assets can well be used with much profit for youngsters who would otherwise have little contact with nature and with the diverse activities of modern industry—but who ought to know about it all and would love it. These contacts can well be organized in a way that would not become a nuisance to the management of the woods, farms, or plants involved.

The impact of urbanization in its present form on American society is full of opportunities which could be beneficial in terms of the education and recreation of children and

youth. It is however also full of dangerous pitfalls if some
of the technical consequences of urban living are allowed to
run wild. The street traffic needs and gets strict regulation,
especially in neighborhoods densely populated with children.
A number of other safety devices and rules have to be adopted
and applied since adults cannot expect from children more
knowledge and responsibility than they have had the time to
acquire. The time left to teen-agers for leisure has been on
the increase as the school programs have been lightened in
many cases and as fewer of them work full time; this leisure
time needs direction and opportunity to use it properly.
Failure to provide these may cause more trouble on city
streets than on scattered farms. In short, urbanization may
be held as one of the factors which create need for more and
more care and planning by parents. Technological progress
may simplify in some ways the adults' tasks but adds new
burdens to their responsibilities.

The New Frontier

It may well be claimed that urbanization has created for
today and for some time ahead a new frontier for the American people to explore and to manage. This new frontier is
not simply one of civilization advancing against the wilderness, a struggle with an environment of an unknown nature,
but rather the reconstruction and continuous improvement
of the areas overrun by modern urban growth. It is the urban
renewal in the heart of old cities, the revitalizing of the
declining suburbs in the "gray zone," the building of new
suburbs, the management of the green areas left in the

vicinity of the metropolises. Cities age as they grow, and the task seems one of almost constantly rejuvenating the vast urban regions in which congregate most of the population. This is a frontier left by the past, which the present must not misuse; it is an essential modern aspect of the permanent struggle of mankind for a better and brighter world to live in. A nation engaged upon it can hardly stop on the way without serious prejudice to the next generation; the frontier must be pushed ahead with the needs of the younger section of the population in mind. The sooner the youth can be associated with this great task, the better it will be, for it is a consuming endeavor but one yielding great rewards.

In this great work of expanding and rejuvenating vast urban regions, the United States is today more advanced than any of the other countries in the world. All these countries, with the exception of very few backward lands, feel the impact of on-rushing urbanization. It is a major concern in the U.S.S.R. and Canada, in Britain and Germany, the Netherlands and France, Italy and Denmark, Mexico and Brazil— even the government of Southern Rhodesia has found it necessary to appoint a Commission on Urban Affairs. Many experts and authorities throughout the world are deeply interested in this new facet of the American experiment. They may well look at the impact urban growth will have on the children and youth of America, and especially those in the large metropolitan areas of the Northeast, as a laboratory from which to learn.

Although such attention will be, and is already focused on these areas it does not follow that local solutions or experiments will be easily copied or duplicated. Every student of urban affairs knows how different is every urban area in the practical handling of its problems, and in the possible attempts at solution. Within the United States alone these differences have already proven great. What is true of New York does not necessarily apply to Philadelphia, certainly not to Washington, and even less to Los Angeles. San Francisco and New Orleans are deeply different in almost every aspect of their urban and metropolitan problems, and so are Houston and Kansas City. Each can and must learn from the experience of the others but it must always put the knowledge thus acquired into the local or regional mold before any consequences can be deduced.

Just because urban growth multiplies along a street houses which look alike on the outside does not mean that it standardizes the people who live in them. Urbanization in fact probably brings more variety, movement, and turmoil to society than was ever expected. These processes must be recognized, their great variety respected and turned into a better system of cooperation and comfort among people. It seems important at this stage that the youth of today be given a hopeful outlook about the city of tomorrow.

THE PLACE OF RELIGION IN AMERICAN LIFE

by MSGR. RAYMOND J.
GALLAGHER
RABBI MARC H. TANENBAUM
and the
REV. DR. WILLIAM J.
VILLAUME

FROM the very beginning of our nation's existence religion has occupied a central place. Belief in the Deity was more than a profession of faith. It found its place in the living experience of Americans. It was not a metaphysical principle that needed demonstration or proving. It was generally accepted as the ground of moral decision for facing all of life's affairs. Belief in God and its consequent responsibilities formed the keystone upholding the arch of national existence. The agenda of goals adopted by the Founding Fathers bears out convincingly their belief in God. Their

The Very Rev. Msgr. Raymond J. Gallagher is Assistant Director, Catholic Charities, Cleveland Diocese. Rabbi Marc H. Tanenbaum is Executive Director of the Synagogue Council of America. The Rev. Dr. William J. Villaume is Executive Director, Department of Social Welfare, Division of Christian Life and Work, National Council of Churches of Christ in the United States of America.

greatest hope for success in the bold ventures they con-
templated was derived from their belief in His existence and
their confidence that under His providence man could develop in honor and in dignity. Society, it seemed to them,
was intimately dependent upon religion.

While revolutionary movements on the continent of Europe were threatening to destroy the influence of religion
on public life, our Founding Fathers based their own revolutionary action on the rights inherent in man as a creature
of God and placed their trust in His divine providence. The
concept of man which they set forth in the Declaration of
Independence was essentially a religious concept. Human
equality stemmed from the fact that all men had been created by God who endowed them equally with rights.

Freedom, too, is essentially bound up with the religious
concept of man. There can be no genuine or lasting freedom
in any context that separates men from the creative and
sustaining God. The enjoyment of all human rights is possible only in a society which acknowledges the supreme and
omnipotent God. Government dedicated to the general welfare is derived from the religious concepts of man and society grounded in the Judeo-Christian tradition.

The early colonists treasured the convictions which they
had salvaged from their previous experiences. Through the
many upheavals of governments which marked the growth of
European nations from the Judeo-Christian traditions, the
basic belief in God had survived. While different governments rose and fell, while significant events left their impres-

sion on history, the basic relationships between man and God endured and proved their lasting value.

The Founding Fathers believed that the lineage of man could be traced back to a creative act of God. From this fact stem the rights and the duties of man. They understood that the essential worth of the human being is based upon his creation in the image of God. Man was considered a living reproduction capable of improving and sharpening the likeness through a life of prayer and godly works, words and deeds. They believed that the essential relationships in life are fashioned after the primary relationship of man to God. This conception set the high level of responsibility between government and the governed. The seriousness of the task and the sacredness of responsible programs are apparent to one who is aware that he is performing a task as a representative of the authority of God. Loyalty, responsibility, and dedication characterize his performance. The commerce and the national economy of such a people is necessarily based upon fairness, honesty, and reliability because both parties to a bargain understand their common identity as creatures of God. Every man's word can be accepted as his bond and his testimony as truthful when citizens acknowledge the fatherhood of God which all enjoy.

In brief summary of these paragraphs about our country's origin, it can be said that part of the bone and sinew of early America was its firm belief in God. Undoubtedly our readers are aware of instances when this simple statement of truth was not a matter of fact. We recognize that exceptions have existed. However, there is no doubt but that the United States is essentially a nation which grew out of convictions as to man's individual honor, freedom, and dignity, and these convictions were based on religion.

Children of God

The development of family life in early American tradition reflected the strong and positive influences that flowed from the biblical tradition. Respectful acceptance of the role of parent by the child and the reverent acceptance of the task of protecting and guiding children constituted the pillars upon which strong and closely knit family life developed. As set forth in the Scriptures the natural primacy of the father in the family was delicately delineated. His role as the good provider, protector, and mentor became the hallmark of a solid American family. Complementary to this position was the sincere honor and respect in which the mother was held. Duties and responsibilities, rights and privileges, meshed into a workable plan for the family.

Based on the traditions of religion whereon single and common lives were lived, marriage was considered to be a sanctified state, not simply a matter of natural instinct and desirability. Marriage offered an opportunity for the happiness of life and for the fulfillment of one's being as a parent, but more than that it offered an opportunity to share in the awesome privilege of creation. Parent and child relationships took their form and fiber from the fact that they were in a natural sequence whereby God placed under the care of parents this living image of their sanctified love.

Familiarity with the Scriptures supported parents in their determination to provide a proper setting for the whole being—body, mind, and spirit. Thus parents so acted as to prepare their children for the worship of God, constructive service to humanity, and individual fulfillment through a godly way of life.

A notable early American attitude toward children was the common conviction that each child had a responsibility for the future. Children were considered as more than mere links in a genealogy. If traditions were to be transmitted from one generation to the next, children had to become familiar with them and imbued with their importance. In the Jewish and Christian traditions, children and youth were considered the guarantors of tomorrow. Today's ideals and goals were not milestones upon which man could rest satisfied. Today's ideals would become tomorrow's achievements through the children who were pathways through a series of tomorrows.

The first born male child, whose uniqueness is clearly set forth in the biblical writings, occupied a position of prominence, importance, and responsibility. His conception of future responsibility would be the measure of family progress. In the early American family the eldest son was faced with the harsh realities of life at a very early early age so that the fearlessness and determination necessary to overcome obstacles would be thoroughly developed within him.

In the early stages of our country's history there was a close partnership between family practices and religious services in church and synagogue. Religious observances in the family began with morning prayer. Grace before meals was standard practice. Bible reading, participated in by the entire family, took place every evening. And on Sabbath and the religious holidays the family engaged in special worship. The table was an altar, the home a sanctuary in which God's presence was felt.

Progress and Change under God

The import of our words until now has been to the effect that religion played a vital role in the formation of our nation and in the generation of our families. A fair appraisal of circumstances as they now exist would indicate that considerable change has taken place. In the progress which we have enjoyed as a nation new interpretations have been placed upon the role of religion in American life. These have resulted in slightly changed and varied approaches but they have left unaltered the essence of the problem. It is probably true to say that America is coming of age and in the process is consolidating within its national identity many new, as well as traditional, ideas. Generally, America today enjoys a great deal more freedom, particularly intellectual freedom. Personal freedom has always been a mark of American society and with the extension of our frontiers and the development of many new areas of activity, intellectual freedom has become more widespread. All aspects of life are studied and analyzed. The communication of news has enjoyed a phenomenal development so that opportunity for analysis and comparison of ideas is now considerably advanced. Religion, among other foundations of the individual's life, must now face openly the test of competition from other values and other plans of life.

People feel they have a right to know the facts and a right to make a decision privately before they are expected to give a statement of their personal position. This democratic approach to knowledge is extended in the field of religion so that many individuals take an inquiring point of view in contemplating the application of religious principles to their private lives.

There is a fringe of extremism present in many of these judgmental activities. It is truthful to say that with regard to religion there is a minor segment of our population which is unbelieving. The place of religion is in no way threatened by them. It is logical to conclude that just as religion endured the upheaval of the world's history until now, it will continue to present a stable way of life to those who take the time to study it thoroughly and apply it in detail to their own life situations.

Another phenomenon in American life which has affected the role of religion is the mobility of individuals and the quickness of the life which they lead. The process of change is so accelerated as to discourage man from the meditative consideration of human existence. In the case of those who have judged it to be essential and who have provided sufficient time to consider the matter, the sound and practical role of religion in their lives has continued.

Educational opportunities have been offered to the broadest segment of the population. These, too, have a broadening effect on the horizons of life and have produced a more knowing appraisal of the institutions and symbolisms of life. Many who have thrilled to the exhilaration of intellectual freedom have misjudged the swing of the pendulum of credibility. Because the gaining of knowledge has had the effect of disproving many false notions, some have rejected those traditional institutions, such as religion, when they could find little in the pragmatic sciences to support religious forms and creeds. True knowledge finds its foundation in a variety of sources, and the mature student of religion has been able to maintain his religious convictions in the face of new scientific data.

In view of the developmental change which we have noted above, it is valid to raise questions at this point. Since many Americans are expressing their concern for the stability of the future, is it not reasonable to say that America is at another crucial point of decision?

America has succeeded in its struggle for identity. Our people were consumed by the fervor of forging a nation in the shortest possible time. They experienced the fever of conquest which led them to challenge the power of mountains, forests, and rivers to stay the hand of their progress. The United States has enjoyed a singular victory over ignorance and has upheld the right of man to know the truth and to enjoy the freedom of applying the truth. The United States has tested its right to endure. Militarily, we have engaged in battles from skirmishes to global conflicts. We have suffered through days of minimal material provisions, through days of sufficiency, regressing through depressions, then moving on to a point of national affluence. The

United States has emerged from diplomatic infancy to the stature of world leadership sworn to achieve the betterment of all peoples. It would not be an inappropriate description to say that America considers itself as having a mission to the world—ideals, goals, standards of living, and standards of performing which we hold so dear and which we agree are based upon religious foundations.

Now we stand on the threshold of the future where things basic to our nation are being challenged. An opposing philosophy of society is poised on the other side of the globe, challenging the worth and the endurance of the spiritual, cultural, and political essence of America. Perhaps more seriously, we are faced with the prospect of moving out of the comfortable limits of our globe into the uncharted universe. Will the present, current version of traditional American attitudes toward God, religious convictions, and value systems be sufficient to meet these tests?

In progressing into the unknown the United States might well formulate its plan in terms of tried and tested truths. As the United States stands at the beginning of another decade, it also faces the beginning of another era. It will aid us substantially if we seek an opportunity to assess the traditional religious concepts in American life and affirm their place in the foundation of American life for the future.

God as Our Goal

People of religious convictions believe that the quest for God and knowledge of His Kingdom are the main purposes of life. Material things, important as they are toward the perfecting of life, are but means to an end. Reaffirmation of belief in authentic spiritual values deserves a priority on the agenda of Americans at this crucial moment in history. The time would seem to be most propitious. Membership rolls of the three major faiths in America are larger than ever before in our history. However casual or superficial the commitment of this membership might be in some instances, it is at least an indication of the concern which families have for insuring a religious component in their lives. They wish to be identified with religious ideals and activities. Churches and synagogues would be derelict in their duty if they did not respond to the promise and opportunity for spiritual greatness which this phenomenon presents.

Religious institutions should be their own severest critics as to the manner and technique in which they present their spiritual message and promote their religious programs. Outmoded, ingrown, unrealistic methodologies should give way to those modern techniques which will keep pace with the phenomenal development of other areas of communication, new information, and knowledge. The closest cooperation among major faiths and sects should be developed. Pointless differences which now dissipate the strength of religious influence in our community should be analyzed and eliminated when their true identity becomes known. It is possible to give substantial emphasis to those basic considerations upon which all agree. Churches and synagogues standing together publicly on fundamental issues can multiply their effectiveness by combating the inroads of irreligion. Cooperation without concession or compromise is clearly possible for the major religious groups in the United States. Too long have we been concerned with protecting what we have, thus blinding ourselves to the advances we could make together.

If the church is to become a genuine force for good in the community, it must harken back to the example given by the best experience of the churches and synagogues in colonial days. These houses of worship were not only the centers of religious and social life but were also the places of leadership and community action. A similar need exists today. A community should look to its qualified leaders for advice and counsel in the decisive areas of life. The manner in which churches and synagogues act in concert to take on the leadership role in community life permits them to contribute greatly to the welfare of all of the nation's citizens. Moral standards, religious practices, delineations of value systems, these are their chief responsibility. Keeping aflame the love of God and fellowmen, inspiring community service, and upholding concepts and ideals which have a spiritual foundation—these are the responsibility of dynamic and fearless leadership on the part of men and women of religious convictions. It is the least the institutions of religion can contribute to a nation which has made possible the unprecedented blessings of religious freedom and toleration. It is the most essential contribution they can make to America as it faces the uncertainty of the future.

Many aspects of community life affecting children and youth can benefit from the introduction, rebirth, or perfecting of existing principles of religion. The degrees in which religion exists in the following facets of community life is at

best inaccurately known and consequently no broad indict-
ment or endorsement can be given.

In labor, the place of religion is fundamental. Churches
and synagogues must look to the development of a sense
of community responsibility so that the common good will
be held above personal gains of either labor or management.
According to the best religious traditions labor has dignity
in itself. The spiritual satisfactions of honest labor and management are ofttimes lost sight of by reason of greed for
success, money, and power. Honesty in the use of time, tools,
materials, and capital by employers and employees is an application of religious principles to a practical purpose. Religious principles of justice, fairness in a day's pay and a
day's work must stand as countervailing influences against
those forces which would demean the high calling and purpose of labor.

The application of law to the lives of individual citizens
is most acceptable when it involves principles drawn from
religion. The law of the land is considered a sharing of the
dominion of God over all mankind. As God's laws are made
for the benefit of the governed, so present day legislators and
other elected officials must be reminded of the attributes of
justice tempered by mercy, which are of the Divine Law-
giver. Honesty, prudence, fairness and justice are but a few
of the moral virtues which describe the true servant of the
law. Service for the sake of others and not for self-aggrandize-
ment is the qualification of those who would serve their
community and their Creator through the practice of the law.

Government currently takes many roles in fulfilling responsibility to the governed. Maintenance of justice and order, leadership in meeting common problems, balance between collective and individual interests and needs are appropriate examples. When the concept of authority is being applied government acts out the role of the father of the greater community. All the noble qualities which apply to the ideal father in the family are pertinent here. Courage of conviction, leadership, judicious use of authority, bravery and dedication, self-sacrifice in the interest of others are all characteristic of the spiritual foundation which must be the basis of the government's service to the governed.

The contribution which love makes to the life of every individual is conditioned by the virtue and godliness which accompanies it. Every aspect of love, whether it be regard, respect, affection, or emotional and physical attraction exemplifies a fundamental virtue. By recognizing and turning to the religious sources of this human experience the community and the individual citizen will be sustained through the sanctity of this basic treasure. The preservation of the religious concept of love thy neighbor as thyself can help overcome indifference, blighting cynicism, or outright baseness of life in society, both governmental and familial.

In the field of education the goal is to prepare our children and youth to live full and creative lives. Careful consideration must be given to building sound moral character as well as to competency in the skills. Both public and private schools have a vital role to play in strengthening the life of the children and youth of America.

Another area where the application of traditional reli-

gious principles would serve the nation is that of amusement
and recreation. We speak here in behalf of self-imposed
standards of excellence. Within the ranks of those who promote amusement, recreation, and entertainment there are
large numbers of nobly motivated, morally concerned people.
Within these same ranks are a few who seek to profit by
the use of subterfuge and legal deceptions. If the industry
itself would identify those who, with malice aforethought,
propagate examples of low moral conduct through theatrical
presentations, through motion pictures, and through printed
pages and pornographic magazines, a great service would be
done the industry and the nation. Discipline from within
would restore confidence in good motives and high moral
purposes and would identify the profiteers for what they are,
those who would capitalize upon protections available to
them.

Parents and families have a distinct role to play in the
re-establishing or the perfecting of moral standards, religious convictions, and ideals. Reconstituting themselves as
the primary teaching unit and basing their instruction on
the eternal verities which have withstood the test of time,
parents can contribute to favorable circumstances wherein
their children can realize their greatest potential. If there
is no concerted and unified effort by parents to close ranks
against the disorganizing force of modern urban society,
they are menacing their children by handicapping them as
well as creating an antagonistic society. It is true that the
absence of citizen attention ofttimes permits the development of negative characteristics in the society in which their

children move and live. The most direct contribution which they can make to the development of ideal circumstances for their children is to create and live by those standards of conduct, those value systems and ideals which lead to an improved citizenry. Once having accepted a code of behavior they should abide by it with great resolution. Once having made a decision about the practical value of this way of life, let them avoid those instances of self-exemption which only serve to confuse the child who watches the performance.

Taking a page from the practice of pioneer families, parents are urged to return to the observance of family religious practices. Family prayer has been promoted widely in the United States in recent years with encouraging results. It is not sufficiently promoted, however, to have a telling result on the spiritual climate of our society. The reading of the Scriptures by the members of the family presents a doubly favorable impression. Presenting the counsel of God through the pages of Scripture will not be lost on the minds of children who are looking for a way of life with authoritative endorsement. Worshiping as a family unit in churches and synagogues contributes to the integrity of the family. This, in turn, enables its children to withstand those forces which are contrary to family standards because of the godly strength which accrues to family standards through family worship.

Respectful observance of religious seasons, feasts, and festivals is another method of incorporating religious convictions and value systems in American life. Incorporating in every such observance an appropriate expression and commentary on the sacredness of the event and its symbolism will add to the impression which the child carries into the future. Above all, those practices which will deepen the convictions for our belonging to this congregation or that organization are of paramount importance. So often we are perplexed by the fact that children of well-regulated families, families which belong to all of the "right" organizations, still succumb to the ways of delinquency. Possibly we are content with mere superficial belonging and do not graft or ingrain into ourselves the basic ideals for which the faith or the organization stands.

The child's role in making these ideals, values, and standards workable is most essential. His complete trust in the leadership of well-motivated parents will contribute in the largest measure to his own fulfillment as an adult and inheritor of the future. In his educational and avocational work his fidelity to honesty, industry, and ambition should be etched on his service record. In his membership in the community, respect for authority as administered by elected and appointed officials will easily be given when it is based on his understanding of their responsibility in the affairs of the community. In his neighborhood his respect for his neighbor's rights and property will be compatible with his drive for property of his own. Kindliness, courtesy and good manners, helpfulness, these are the marks of one who has triumphed over the smallness and narrowness which sometimes captures human beings. A charitable concern for each neighbor, his home and his family, a respectful acceptance of differences in race, creed, and national origin, these are the marks of a youth who has truly inherited the tradition of America.

In his family he should have respect for his parents and the authority vested in their office as well as respect for authority vested in those who take the parents' place. This constitutes the surest guarantee of his ability to assume responsibilities as he grows through the years. A reverence for the union which binds his parents together and a fervent hope that his future will be similarly blessed, this describes a youth who understands his responsibility as a guarantor of the future.

In his private life, that which the child alone forms, his communion with God and his generous attitude toward other people are the foundation stones upon which his personal integrity is based. With religious nurture and experience a child emerges to a point of adult responsibility with honesty, justice, mercy, patriotism, modesty, loyalty, courage, bravery, and a sense of service to his fellowman often beyond the mere call of duty. Such a youth, despite whatever faces him and his country, is well prepared to deal successfully with the challenges that are ahead.

Conclusion

The foregoing has attempted to describe the place of religion in American life. The foundation which religion gives the standards, value systems, and ideals we treasure has been set forth in simple narrative without any effort to deal with the subject as a theological or an historical treatise. The attempt has succeeded if it has reminded those who seek guidance for the decade of the 1960s that the golden thread of religion woven through the tapestry of American history has served the nation well.

Material values alone tend towards diminishing returns, total lifelessness, and decay. People who live by them only are trying to perpetuate things which of their very mundane nature cannot be perpetuated. They cling to objects and values which time destroys without mercy. They are bound up in a contingent and material order of things, customs, clothes, architecture, places, and personalities which inevitably change and give way to something else.

We cannot bequeath to our children that which will crumble in the very act of possessing. We must consider our responsibilities unmet until we have included in the blueprint of our current American life those lasting values which will endure beyond the inevitable changes which face our children and the universe in which they will live.

THE NEW LEISURE

by AUGUST HECKSCHER

THE CHANGES which have occurred in American life over the past decade are cumulative and interwoven, so that it is difficult to make any one of them predominant or to single one out as the principal cause of others. The increase in the size of families, the move away from the center of the cities, the decline of inter-urban transportation, the increased proportion of young people making college their goal—these are all part of one picture. For purposes of study or action we may isolate one aspect or another. But as observers of social change, we must accept these and other factors as closely interrelated. In ways which can often be discussed only generally, these various developments react upon each other. Each stimulates the total movement and gives an impetus to the direction in which the social order tends to move.

If we were to look for a single change underlying others, however, we would have to give close attention to leisure. Today's child is growing up in a period marked by an emphasis on the values of leisure and a growing amount of

August Heckscher is Director of the Twentieth Century Fund.

leisure time. In no other force making for change has there been involved so deep a transformation of values, of philosophy, and of ethics. The United States was founded under the inspiration of religious and secular codes which gave primary emphasis to the place of work in a man's life. A job was related to the Puritan concept of a "calling"; and a "calling" was related to man's destiny both in this world and the next. The result was a striking capacity to accomplish material goals, but this was accompanied by the danger that the sources of cultural life might dry up. At its best Puritanism infused work with spiritual quality. But when this failed, as it did in time, the husk of materialism was left, and people spent their lives in work which had less and less inner meaning.

For various reasons the emphasis on work declined as the twentieth century advanced. Hours on the job were steadily reduced from approximately sixty in 1900 to an average of forty in 1950. Often, this occurred as part of a movement to "share the work" or as a tactic for gaining more "overtime"—the former in the depression, the latter in periods of prosperity. But there has been a genuine desire for a shorter working day, and this has been accomplished and combined with lengthened vacations for everyone, as well as a longer span of retirement extended even further by the added years contributed by medical science. In the period ahead we shall undoubtedly see the work week further shortened. It should not be overlooked, however, that people expect a continually higher standard of living, which means that a good portion of the gains in productivity—roughly two-

thirds over the past decades—tend to be assigned to the output of more goods rather than the enjoyment of more free
time.

Whatever the forms or the precise amount of leisure time
which may accrue over the next decade, the fact is plain that
a revolution has occurred in American values. No longer
does work hold undisputed sway at the center of life. It may
be a matter of debate as to what rivals it, or has taken its
place. Travel, the family, improvement of the home, civic
and cultural activities—each of these and others could make
their claim. For the moment it is enough to suggest that the
energizing focus of the individual's life has altered or been
diffused; and this has led to dramatic changes throughout
the whole social system.

The move to the suburbs, for example, is related to the
new values of a leisure civilization. Men and women are
getting away physically from the scene of their labors to an
environment where a host of new interests and problems
preoccupy them. The growing predominance of the private
car in place of the instruments of mass transportation is
likewise part of the new approach. In automobiles men
seek the freedom and independence that have traditionally
been associated with leisure pursuits.

Now such trends often defeat their real purpose. The preoccupations of suburban life come to exert a tyranny of their
own; the long journey to and from work eats into the sup-
posedly free hours of the day; the automobile immobilized
in traffic becomes a symbol of the futility of man's effort
to escape into a realm of freedom. We need to evaluate

critically many of the forms and methods the country has adopted as a consequence of the decline of a work-centered civilization. But despite many frustrations and dead ends we are witnessing a search for genuine leisure. In the process of that search our institutions and habits are being made over.

The Impact on Youth

The life of children and young people in such a period of social change is bound to be deeply affected. Children are sensitive to a surprising degree to shifts in the winds of doctrine about them. The family may like to think of itself as a watertight unit, maintaining its own standards regardless of the world outside. But this is an illusion. The society of which we are all a part exerts an extraordinarily pervasive force. Parents brought up amid the economies of a depression may try to maintain among their children the habits of austerity and self-help which were among the rewarding features of that era. They find this to be an almost impossible task. The children are of their own time; its standards and tendencies speak to them compellingly.

How alert children are to the forces of the time may be seen by observing those families which do not own television. Despite its absence in the home the children will have picked up the language, the familiar images, the whole flavor of the TV age. It is as if their minds were peculiarly sensitized to their own period and armed against whatever is carried over or imposed by authority.

It is natural, therefore, that so profound a change as is

represented by the growth of leisure values should have caught on among the younger generation. How it has affected them is not easy to determine. The first answer would be that it has made them, like their elders, "leisure-minded," or especially concerned with recreational activities. But that would be an oversimplification. The essential point about youth is that, while absorbing and being influenced by the world of their elders, they inhabit very largely a world of their own. The communications between these two worlds are direct and continuous, but the messages arrive at their destinations in a distorted and sometimes incomprehensible form. There seems to be no doubt, for instance, that many of the behavior patterns which we describe under the name of "delinquency" are an effort on the part of the young to communicate something important to the adult group. Similarly, the adult communications on the subject of leisure reach the mind of youth in a garbled form.

The reason for this is that work and leisure have meanings of their own for children, often significantly at variance with those held by the rest of the population. In its most dramatic form this difference can be pointed out by the fact that the Greek word for leisure, *scola*, is essentially the same as our word for school. "What!" we can hear some young student exclaiming, "You mix up a word meaning fun and freedom and recreation with this word which speaks to us of toil and bondage. You have the audacity to suggest that when we're at school we're not working—that we're actually resting and enjoying ourselves!" Without stopping to ask how this strange derivation arose, we make for

the moment the simple point that a child's concept of
work, like a child's concept of leisure, is not the same as the
philosopher's. It is by no means identical with the activities
which the adult would place under these categories. (It
should be added, incidentally, that not all adults agree as
to what they consider leisure as opposed to work.)

Much of what we call "play" for children is undertaken
seriously, in an entirely workmanlike manner. When children play they are preparing for the roles they will be called
on to assume in later life. They imitate what they cannot
yet comprehend, they play at "mothers" or "shopkeepers" or
"soldiers" as the spirit moves them and as the fashions of
the grown-up world suggest. In childhood the difference between work and play is not marked; even when they do
something which their parents consider useful, such as setting the table or raking leaves, they still see themselves engaged in an imitation of adult behavior. If they grumble
under what they affect to be a tyrannical imposition, that
is also part of the game. They assume that such a reaction
is expected of them. Have they not observed their elders
giving vent to just such emotions?

The significant change which may be expected in these
early years is not, therefore, more "leisure." It is play built
around somewhat different patterns and preoccupations.
The decline in the relative importance of the job as the
adult criterion of status and prestige will mean that the
children shift the objects of their imitation. The types of
toys put on the market and their degrees of popularity
should provide to the researcher an interesting test of the

hypothesis presented here. Do the children organize their group around the image of a country club, instead of the image of an army? Do they put more emphasis on the simulated family than the simulated shop?

The Teen-Ager

In older children we begin to see more clearly the effect of a leisure oriented society upon youth. In the early teens, or perhaps before, the young person begins to make a very sharp distinction between work and play. We would expect, therefore, to see the element of play stressed to a degree that would have surprised earlier generations. This appears to be the case. The parents cannot but become more permissive toward their children as they relax for themselves the rigorous standards of an older code. The children cannot but become more inclined to take things easy. It may be difficult to document the change, but the fact seems to be that in terms of foot-pounds of energy the present generation of young people does not make the same expenditure as its predecessors. They do not walk as far; it is impossible to imagine them undertaking regularly a trip of even a few miles on foot to school. It is questionable whether they devote themselves with the same degree of application to intellectual tasks and studies. Memory exercises have gone out of fashion. As the emphasis on work diminishes, the young people turn to play and recreation with an avidity patterned on the behavior of their elders.

A shift in the school curriculum away from the classical and general studies toward more vocational subjects may be seen as one of the results of the leisure-minded society. The classical studies almost always require a high level of concentration as well as a dedication to work for its own sake. They deal with matters outside the immediate interests of the student. Their relevance is not evident at first glance and their best rewards are often deferred. In contrast, the vocational studies are easily assimilated and bring direct benefits.

The shift away from the classics in the school curriculum has, however, its paradoxical side. A society oriented toward leisure—at least toward leisure as it has been understood by past societies—would be expected to shun vocationalism. It would teach young people the values and pursuits which make it possible for a man or woman in later life to draw for enjoyment upon inner resources. The more practical emphasis in the curriculum has usually been associated with a life given over early and exclusively to a job. Actually, however, the vocational courses of today are frequently leisure-oriented. Not only do they require relatively little effort; they are bent to what are called "leisure skills." Thus automobile driving and automobile care are directly related to the aim of every high-school student to own a car at the earliest possible moment. One cannot help asking whether leisure skills can or should be isolated from the broader aims of education. And if they are to be the goal, is not the most important of them all a capacity to read with concentration and understanding?

In our society, in brief, vocationalism in education is often not associated with work, but with recreation. General studies, which should form the basis of a leisure-minded education, are neglected, in part because of the toil and sweat which their pursuit requires.

The curriculum is not the only part of school life affected by the trend toward leisure. The whole atmosphere of the school, its official and nonofficial extra-curricular activities, are influenced by what is going on in the life of the community around it. The architecture of the newer schools, which has certainly made them bright and cheerful, reflects the standards of the modern shopping center, or even of the modern place of work. The gymnasium and auditorium stand out prominently; wide corridors, courtyards, sheltered areas combine to impress upon the student a feeling that what goes on outside the classroom—the conversations, the friendly contacts, the periods of relaxation—are as important as what goes on within the classroom itself.

Beyond the high school, education also derives its atmosphere in large part from the same standards. College work has certainly become more demanding as a result of the heightened competition and the press of numbers; it may well be that a new seriousness is today setting the tone. But it is the seriousness, not of the traditional higher learning, but of the modern community—the modern suburban community. It is interesting to note to what degree the college campus has actually adopted the values and behavior patterns of the suburb. Coeducation and student marriages create interests which are oriented toward the personal and subjective, rather than toward that objective truth which was the aim of older education. The extra-curricular activities tend to become social in nature, rather than to be patterned on the battle field or the political forum. The curriculum is infused with the same values. History, for example, is viewed less as the actions of strong men, the creation of human will, than the result of impersonal trends and processes. Even the manner of teaching is affected. Wherever possible the old lecture course is abandoned in favor of the small group or seminar. The professor, instead of standing forth as a public figure, is like the leader of a congenial group of conversationalists during the coffee hour.

The fear once was that the college, instead of being a place apart, would become infected by the standards of the market place. The market place has declined in its appeal in an age of leisure. The new danger is that the college will be infected by the standards of suburban living.

Leisure and Consumption

The standards of a leisure society have further influenced young people by making them conscious of their role as consumers. Leisure as we understand it in the United States has little to do with the contemplative or passive mood. Reading may be a part of leisure, yet it is generally reading for self-improvement or reading which personally involves the individual, permitting him to escape from his normal circumstances into a realm of action or romance. Movies and television seem to be watched as a means to vicarious experience, not with a critical and disinterested spirit. In short, even those activities which on the surface appear passive are really a substitute for action, while action in palpable and vigorous forms provides the content of most leisure hours. Men and women boat, golf, ski, garden, bowl—and in innumerable other ways prove that they are devotees of what the advertisers like to call "active leisure."

As a result, leisure in the United States is an expensive commodity. It is not simply that people stop earning money when they leave the factory or office; they begin spending it at an increased rate. Common sense would tell us that this leads to a painful dilemma: if men want to enjoy their free time they must work more in order to make more money —but if they work more, then they do not have the free time. Fortunately certain economic factors come into play to rescue the leisure-minded individual from so impossible a situation. The process is something like this: The goods, services, and equipment which are consumed by the population in their free time create a vast demand which can only be met by the introduction of more efficient machines. These machines permit the production of constantly greater amounts in a given period—so much so that the worker, through the blessings of advanced technology, can earn more and have both his goods and his leisure. It is a beneficent process, but if it is to work it means that the population must live up to its role of consumers. It could not, even if it wished, content itself with the role of observers or philosophers.

The social ethic of consumerism puts its mark on younger people. Brought up in a period of prosperity and abundance they would be ready in any case to demand what they conceive to be their share of material goods. The large amount of uncommitted time which naturally falls to them increases this disposition. The "teen-age market" is a rich target for the merchant and advertiser. Even the younger children, whose material desires do not extend beyond the possession of a few toys, are sought as agents to influence the parents. Thus from the beginning leisure is colored by the tendency to link it with the buying of gadgets and the spending of money.

There is, of course, another quality of leisure; indeed the word has been associated in other periods with a passive rather than an active mood. The leisured aristocrat might have estates and costly ceremonies as the background against which his days of idleness were lived. But within this elaborate frame his pursuits were simple. Often, as in hunting or yachting, he deliberately recreated the conditions of a simpler, less mechanized existence. For the rest, his major delights were conversation, love-making, gossip, dancing, visiting, theater-going, and reading.

When leisure is of this kind an affinity exists between the way children and grown-ups spend their free time. For children in their natural state are also wanderers and gossipers, and pass the hours of the day without need for specific occupations or elaborate equipment. The play of younger children is not, it is true, as unstructured as it may appear to the outsider. What gives the impression of being endless and undifferentiated in the activities of an afternoon may involve for the participants a series of more or less definite periods, each with its own form and content. Yet in general children behave not unlike their elders in an idle and aristocratic age: when they go somewhere their major destination is "out," and when they do something they feel the best way to describe it is "nothing."

Today the standards of the adult world reach back into the world of children making them less "idle" but also more dependent for their pleasures on the output of the machine technology. These same children will, as they grow up, make the leisure of the future even more "active" and gadget-ridden. In other periods—even today when so much of an older ethic persists—the tendency toward a materialistic use of leisure is softened by habits natural to childhood. Amid the glittering temptations of worldliness the instincts of play remain. Long, unbounded summer days, with their expanses of delicious emptiness, linger in the memory and make it never quite possible to equate leisure with the doing of something formalized and expensive. But in the next generation this pool of simplicity may have been drained dry. Those whose childhood has been surrounded by an avalanche of consumer goods will accept, without saving inhibitions or doubts, the duty of consumption as the price of prosperity and increasing free time.

The Two Worlds

If leisure in the period ahead is to be meaningful, a new relationship must be established between the youthful and adult worlds. It is clear that a new relationship is in fact in the making: leisure has brought parents and children into a state of "togetherness" which is not the mere invention of the phrase-makers. What is not so clear is whether the interaction of these two worlds as it is at present developing will be of benefit to society as a whole. Children may well thrive on a certain degree of salutary neglect—or at least of independence; and as for parents, they certainly do better when they are not tied down completely to the care and entertainment of their offspring. It may be that the adult and youthful groups of the family, each maintaining its own separateness and identity, not only create a happier family life but also a better social order.

It may be asked at this point why "togetherness" and leisure necessarily accompany each other. It would be quite possible to conceive of a state of society in which the husband, released from his work, regularly passed several hours at his club, at sports, at a cafe or bar. This happens, of course. But in American life the normal pattern is for the man to move as rapidly as the commuting facilities allow between the two spheres of home and office. The more free time he has, the more time at home; and the more time at home, the greater the responsibilities he is inevitably compelled to take in the management of the household and the care of the children. The same happens in regard to vacations. The annual paid vacation is equivalent to a guaranteed period of close family life. Travel means travel with all the children.

One of the complicating factors in the growth of free time is, indeed, the necessity of keeping the work week of industry and that of the school geared to each other. Where a four-day week has been tried, a major factor against it has been the inability of the parents to undertake trips or excursions because the children did not share the extra day.

This awkwardness of scheduling is bound to be troublesome, especially if the development of the weekend house becomes as prevalent in the next decade as now seems likely. Of course the children might ask why their hours of work should not be reduced to the same extent as their parents'. Unfortunately increased productivity has not affected the schoolroom as it has the factory; learning, like art accomplishment, is still long. Another way out would be for school to move toward the four-day week in step with industry, making up for the lost time by shortening the summer vacation. This solution, however, would raise problems of its own.

The four-day week does not, as a matter of fact, appear to be in the offing. The labor unions prefer to put the emphasis on longer paid vacations, well aware that many workers would take second jobs during the three-day weekend, thus undermining union loyalty and discipline. Male workers (the women are in a somewhat different position) make this form of additional free time their first choice. The problem of coordinating the leisure of children and grown-ups will nevertheless become a real one in the future; there are many reasons of necessity for keeping family schedules meshed. But there is something to be said also, at least in theory, for keeping them independent of each other, with the parents and the children having at least some free time to themselves.

The arguments against having the father become too intricately involved in the chores of household and child-raising have been persuasively set forth by Margaret Mead and others. With the father so much of the time at home, and so busy helping the mother in her tasks, the sense of a distinct quality of maleness is dimmed; the role of the two sexes is confused, and the basis of paternal authority is undermined. As for the mother, she has, of course, a primary responsibility in this field. But even here the contacts with the children can be too close and continuous, without periods for refreshment, appraisal, or the cultivation of new interests.

The case for the independence of children, in at least a part of their leisure pursuits, can be made with equal weight. If it is necessary, in St. Paul's phrase, "to put away childish things," it is also necessary to have been thoroughly at home among such things in youth. We have already spoken of the quality of play and its importance in the life of the child. What needs to be stressed is how important it is in the life of society as a whole. *Homo Ludens*—Man Playing—is the title of one of the most subtle and profound of all books on leisure. Where the adult world loses the spirit of play there vanishes with it a capacity for disinterestedness, a sense of the meanings that underlie the outward forms of life, a delight in ceremonies and festivals and all the symbolic manifestations which can give to a civilization such color as it has. The instinct for play is deep in the child; but it is stifled or overlaid where grown-up standards are imposed too early. And if it is stifled, society loses one of the vitally important educative forces within it.

It would seem therefore, that as free time increases in our society, that we are going to have to devise means of keeping various elements—and particularly the worlds of young people and of grown-ups—from coalescing. Within the American culture, leisure has tended to mean a coming together, a homogenizing of elements which had once maintained a certain individual character and distinctness. Conformity and leisure have seemed to accompany each other. To counteract this trend our society could well give attention to means for giving young people opportunities for vacations apart from their parents, so that both—parents and children—could find in recreation a fulfillment of their own interests. It could make sure that alternative forms of enjoyment are not neglected under the influence of forces which draw everything tightly toward the home circle—toward the family room, the patio, the barbecue pit, and the private swimming pool. I would suggest that organizations which encourage scouting, skiing groups, wilderness trips, and youthful tourism could be especially useful in the time ahead. They emphasize a kind of recreation not primarily dependent on consumer purchases; they draw young people toward vigorous physical exercise, and remind them of the values which youth holds in common across the world.

The emphasis in this section has been on the necessity for youth to have its own forms of leisure. These forms would be different in many ways from those of adults in a consumer society where individuals, having attained a high degree of equality with each other, seem more than ever concerned with differentiating themselves from others on the basis of this consumption. In stressing this side of the coin I do not want, however, to undervalue the importance of recreational activities undertaken by the family group, or by father and son together. Indeed it is when the older and younger generations have each been allowed a certain measure of freedom and have enjoyed themselves in their own way that they can come together for the truest delights. Togetherness implies a degree of separateness as its base; this is particularly true in the context of American leisure.

The Role of Work

To speak of leisure without speaking of it in relation to work is to give only part of the picture. The simplest definition of leisure time is that part of a man's waking hours which are not given to the job. Even this implies a relationship; for what a man does in his free time is inevitably affected by what he does at his job. Jobs that ask nothing but routine efforts and those that are physically or mentally exhausting are more likely to lead to hours off the job spent purposelessly.

There are elements of a man's work—if the work be not wholly unrewarding—which have in them the qualities of leisure: the sense of voluntary effort, of satisfaction in the accomplishment of a manageable task. The place of work, moreover, is often deliberately designed so as to underline the modern relationship between work and leisure. Some of the newer office buildings, set handsomely in the country, surrounded by gardens and facilities for recreation, are obviously aimed to strike a note of relaxation.

As we think of youth today, we must be a little troubled by the realization of how slightly the image of work impinges on his mind. All around him in the most dramatic and tempting forms are the visible allurements of leisure. He knows his father is away during certain hours of the day, but he has little idea of what he does. A visit to the office may actually increase the wonderment, particularly as the surroundings can appear so agreeable. Meanwhile the more physical forms of man's toil, which in older generations were much in evidence, are hidden behind walls and rarely visited. Under these circumstances it is difficult for the young person to know or feel much about the world of work.

School and college are work of a kind, but they are not the same as a job seriously undertaken by a young person during vacations or during his education and sustained with growing responsibility. A boy's recreation is empty if it is not a contrast to real work; what should be leisure is mere boredom. As already suggested, juvenile delinquency is in part a protest, subconscious and inarticulate, against a society which gives to the rising generation no role which absorbs its energies and focuses its aims.

It is not only the weight of visible and obvious factors in the environment which draws youth away from work; it is the whole sentiment against "child labor," embodied in laws which had once a terrible justification as well as in the mores of a society which looks to a steadily decreasing work load. The tendency for everyone to go through high school, and now for increasing numbers to go through college, is part of this same picture. May it not be, however, that when we come to grapple effectively with the problems of the new leisure we shall retrace some of the steps we have taken in this century. We may well expect youth to enter earlier into the work force and to use the machine's gift of free time for the completion of his training and for liberal studies in subsequent years. Adult education may not only be the answer to the emptiness of so much of the free time which falls to men and women in later life; it may also be the key to restoring to youth an early sense of being part of the world's work.

If youth should thus recapture a sense of work, it would be carried over naturally into the adult years, and the way is opened for a more healthy balance between work and recreation in the whole social order. Here is a final example of what may be described as the central argument of this analysis: that there is a constant interaction between the leisure of the child and the leisure of the grown-up world. The child's play, imaginatively encouraged, creates a spirit which can give to all of his later life a leisurely and humane aspect; it permits the full maturing of the personality, the development of a detached, humorous, and worldly-wise attitude. The grown-up's recreation, on the other hand, can reach backward into the stage of adolescence. If it is a form of recreation dependent on status symbols and the purchase of material objects its effects will inevitably be debasing and narrowing. The adolescents of today, moreover, will be teaching their own children tomorrow, by example and precept, the then accepted patterns of recreation and entertainment.

To a greater degree than in other areas of life, the child teaches the adult as much as the adult teaches the child.

Therefore it is of the utmost importance that the natural disposition of each be developed along sound and creative lines. What may be considered healthy recreation for adults is a large question; but for young people, as we have suggested here, recreation must certainly involve a whole range of activities divorced from the highly organized and materialistic aspects of an industrialized age. They must be activities which keep alive the imagination, or delight in symbols and ceremonies, a love of nature, and a feeling for the endless variety and mystery of human relationships.

SUGGESTED READING

FROM FRONTIER TO SUBURBIA by FOSTER RHEA DULLES

Allen, Frederick Lewis. *The Big Change*. New York, Harper, 1952.
Hofstadter, Richard. *The Age of Reform*. New York, Knopf, 1955.
Knoles, George Harmon. *The New United States*. New York, Holt, 1959.
Lerner, Max. *America As a Civilization*. New York, Simon & Schuster, 1958.
Link, Arthur S. *American Epoch*. New York, Knopf, 1955.

DEMOGRAPHIC TRENDS AND IMPLICATIONS by ELEANOR H. BERNERT

Bernert, Eleanor H. *America's Children*. New York, Wiley, 1958.
Glick, Paul C. *American Families*. New York, Wiley, 1957.
Taeuber, Conrad and Irene B. Taeuber. *The Changing Population of the United States*. New York, Wiley, 1958.

THE AMERICAN FAMILY IN THE PERSPECTIVE OF OTHER CULTURES by CONRAD M. ARENSBERG

Chapple, E. D. and C. S. Coon. *Principles of Anthropology*. New York, Holt, 1942.
LePlay, Frédéric. *Les Ouvriers européens*. Paris, 1885.

Lowie, Robert E. *Social Organization*. New York, Rinehart, 1948.
Murdock, George P. *Social Structure*. Toronto, Macmillian, 1949.
Thomas, W. B., ed. *Man's Role in Changing the Face of the Earth*. Chicago, University of Chicago Press, 1955.

THE AMERICAN FAMILY TODAY by REUBEN HILL

Duvall, Evelyn M. *Family Development*. Chicago, Lippincott, 1957.
LeMasters, E. E. *Modern Courtship and Marriage*. New York, Macmillan, 1957.
Mead, Margaret. *Male and Female: A Study of the Sexes in a Changing World*. New York, Morrow, 1949.
Miller, Daniel R., and Guy E. Swanson. *The Changing American Parent*. New York, Wiley, 1958.
Sirjamaki, John. *The American Family in the 20th Century*. Cambridge, Harvard University Press, 1953.

THE CHANGING NEGRO FAMILY by HYLAN LEWIS

Frazier, E. Franklin. *Black Bourgeoisie*. Glencoe, Ill., Free Press, 1957.
Ginzberg, Eli. *The Negro Potential*. New York, Columbia University Press, 1956.
Merton, Robert K. *Social Theory and Social Structure*. Revised and enlarged edition. Glencoe, Ill., Free Press, 1957.

A HEALTHIER WORLD by GEORGE ROSEN, M.D.

Baker, S. J. *Fighting for Life*. New York, Macmillan, 1939.
Bradbury, D. E. *Four Decades of Action for Children: A Short History of the Children's Bureau*. Washington, D.C., Government Printing Office, 1956.
Duffus, R. L. and L. Emmett Holt, Jr. *L. Emmett Holt: Pioneer of a Children's Century*. New York, Appleton-Century, 1940.

Oliver, W. W. *The Man Who Lived for Tomorrow: A Biography of William Hallock Park, M.D.* New York, E. P. Dutton, 1941.

Rosen, George. *A History of Public Health.* New York, MD Publications, 1958.

Smillie, W. G. *Public Health: Its Promise for the Future.* New York, Macmillan, 1955.

GROWING UP IN AN AFFLUENT SOCIETY by MOSES ABRAMOVITZ

Galbraith, John Kenneth. *The Affluent Society.* New York, Houghton, 1958.

de Tocqueville, Alexis. *Democracy in America.* Corrected and revised by Philips Bradley. New York, Knopf, 1945.

Veblen, Thorstein. *The Theory of the Leisure Class.* 1899.

THE IMPACT OF URBANIZATION by JEAN GOTTMANN

Conant, James B. *The American High School Today: A First Report to Interested Citizens.* New York, McGraw-Hill, 1959.

Duncan, Otis Dudley and Albert J. Reiss, Jr. *Social Characteristics of Urban and Rural Communities.* New York, Wiley, 1950.

Ginzberg, Eli et al. *The Ineffective Soldier,* 3 vols. New York, Columbia University Press, 1959.

Gottmann, Jean. *Virginia at Mid-Century.* New York, Holt, 1955.

THE PLACE OF RELIGION IN AMERICAN LIFE by RAYMOND J. GALLAGHER, MARC H. TANENBAUM, and WILLIAM J. VILLAUME

Bryson, Lyman. *The New America.* New York, Harpers, 1956.

Cohen, Morris Raphael. *American Thought.* Glencoe, Free Press, 1954.

Cousins, Norman. *In God We Trust*. New York, Harpers, 1958.

Gabriel, R. Henry (ed.). *The Pageant of America*. Volume 10. New Haven, Yale University Press, 1928.

Garrison, Winfred. *March of Faith*. New York, Harpers, 1933.

Herberg, Will. *Protestant—Catholic—Jew*. New York, Doubleday, 1955.

Lerner, Max. *America As a Civilization*. New York, Simon and Schuster, 1958.

National Council of Churches of Christ in America, Social Welfare Department. *The Church and Juvenile Delinquency*, by Robert and Muriel Webb. New York, Association Press, 1957.

THE NEW LEISURE *by* AUGUST HECKSCHER

Arendt, Hannah. *The Human Condition*. Chicago, Chicago University Press, 1958.

Bell, Daniel. *Work and Its Discontent*. Boston, Beacon Press, 1958.

Huizinga, Johan. *Homo Ludens*. Boston, Beacon Press, 1955.

Larrabee, Eric and Rolf Meyersohn, eds. *Mass Leisure*. Glencoe, Free Press, 1958.

Veblen, Thorstein. *The Theory of the Leisure Class*. 1899.

Williams, Wayne R. *Recreation Places*. New York, Reinhold, 1958.